Integrated Marketing

Also available in the McGraw-Hill Marketing for Professionals Series:

COMPETITIVE RETAIL MARKETING
Dynamic Strategies for Winning and Keeping Customers
Andrew Collins
ISBN 0 07 707567 6

MANAGING IDEAS FOR PROFIT
The Creative Gap
Simon Majaro
ISBN 0 07 707598 6

VALUE-ADDED MARKETING
Marketing Management for Superior Results
Torsten Nilson
ISBN 0 07 707655 9

CUSTOMER-FOCUSED MARKETING
Actions for Delivering Greater Internal and External Customer Satisfaction
Ian Chaston
ISBN 0 07 707698 2

MARKETING AUDIT CHECKLISTS
A Guide to Effective Marketing Resource Realization
Aubrey Wilson
ISBN 0 07 707760 1

STRATEGIC MARKETING
A European Approach
Jean-Jacques Lambin
ISBN 0 07 707795 4

BRANDING IN ACTION
Cases and Strategies For Profitable Brand Management
Philippa Cowking and Graham Hankinson
ISBN 0 07 707757 1

TARGETING FOR SUCCESS
A Guide to New Techniques for Measurement and Analysis in Database and Direct Marketing
John Ozimek
ISBN 0 07 707766 0

Details of these and other titles in the series are available from:
The Product Manager, Professional Books, McGraw-Hill Book Company Europe, Shoppenhangers Road, Maidenhead, Berkshire SL6 2QL
Telephone 0628 23432 Fax 0628 770224

Integrated Marketing

Making marketing work in industrial and business-to-business companies

Richard N. Skinner

McGraw-Hill Book Company

London · New York · St Louis · San Francisco · Auckland
Bogotá · Caracas · Lisbon · Madrid · Mexico
Milan · Montreal · New Delhi · Panama · Paris · San Juan
São Paulo · Singapore · Sydney · Tokyo · Toronto

Published by
McGraw-Hill Book Company Europe
Shoppenhangers Road, Maidenhead, Berkshire, SL6 2QL, England
Telephone 0628 23432
Fax 0628 770224

British Library Cataloguing in Publication Data
Skinner, Richard N.
Integrated Marketing: Making Marketing
Work in Industrial and Business-to-Business Marketing.—
(McGraw-Hill Marketing for Professionals Series)
I. Title II. Series
658.8

ISBN 0-07-707768-7

Library of Congress Cataloging-in-Publication Data
The cataloging-in-publication data of this title has been logged with the Library of Congress, Washington, DC USA.

12345 CUP 97654

Typeset by BookEns Limited, Baldock, Herts.
and printed and bound in Great Britain at
the University Press, Cambridge.

Contents

Series Foreword

The series title, Marketing for Professionals, was not chosen lightly, and it carries with it certain clear responsibilities for publisher, authors and series advisers alike.

First, the books must actually be intended and written for marketing practitioners. Most, if not all, will undoubtedly serve a valuable purpose for students of marketing. However, from the outset the primary objective of this series is to help the professional hands-on marketer to do his or her job that little (but important) bit better.

In turn, this commitment has helped to establish some basic ground rules: no 'Janet-and-John' first steps for toddlers; no lessons in egg sucking for grandmothers (who these days may have a Business Studies degree); and equally, no withdrawal into the more esoteric and abstruse realms of academe.

It follows that the subject matter of these books must be practical and of topical value to marketers operating – indeed, battling – in today's rapidly evolving and violently competitive business environment. Cases and case material must be relevant and valid for today; where authors deal with familiar marketing tools and techniques, these must be in terms which, again, up-date and adapt them, bringing them as close as possible to what in the current idiom we call the leading edge.

This has set demanding standards but, such is the calibre of authors contributing to the series, perfectly acceptable ones. The authors are either senior marketers or leading consultants and marketing academics with a strong practical background in management. Indeed, a number in both categories (and as the series extends, it is to be hoped, a growing proportion) are themselves members of The Marketing Society, with the pre-requisite level of seniority and experience that implies.

McGraw-Hill Book Company Europe, as professional in its field as the target marketers are in theirs, has consulted The Marketing Society extensively in the search for suitable topics and authors, and in the evaluation and, if necessary, revision of proposals and manuscripts for new additions to the series.

The result is a well presented and growing library of modern, thoughtful and extremely useful handbooks covering eventually all aspects of marketing. It is a library that every marketing professional will want to have on his or her bookshelf. It is also a series with which The Marketing Society is very pleased to be associated, and is equally happy to endorse.

Gordon Medcalf
Director General
The Marketing Society

Preface
Perceptions and misconceptions

Marketing has arrived, or so its chief exponents would have us believe. There is certainly evidence to support such a view. Degrees and diplomas in marketing can be obtained from a number of respected universities and polytechnics, even in a country which has been slow to accept new academic disciplines. Marketing experts are beginning to think, and speak, of themselves as professionals, while lay people outside industry or commerce are quite familiar with the word itself. This growing prominence is reflected in institutions. We have a Chartered Institute of Marketing, with some 50 000 members and students, while in London the Worshipful Company of Marketors is now well established in the list of City Livery Companies.

Yet however frequently the word is used, there are lingering doubts about what it really means, to the general public, to industry and even to some of its practitioners. Official definitions are so wide as to embrace almost all forms of commercial activity. I have no wish to refute these; indeed I shall argue that supplying customers with a product that they want at a profit to the seller is not a function which can be confined to one small corner of a business. Nevertheless what the word normally conveys to people both inside and outside industry is nothing like so wide. For some it is still another word for selling, or perhaps for advertising. If further aspects are admitted, such as market research or product planning or other forms of sales promotion, then marketing becomes a mixed bundle of techniques, which may be applied to increase sales.

A bolt-on extra

Looked at in this way marketing is seen as a bolt-on addition to a business that would be complete in itself without it. Just attach it according to the instructions, and you too can succeed in this harsh world! Those of us who have been called in to advise smaller companies on marketing have frequently been met with amazement and disappointment if it has been suggested that the product range, or pricing policy, or the way the entire firm is managed should be re-examined. 'No, no, what we want to know is how to sell more. Just give us a few ideas.'

Another disturbing aspect of marketing, if it is to be regarded as an established discipline, is that it is often seen to fail. Large and small companies alike fall short of their marketing objectives and run into serious financial trouble. When the magic has not worked there is an inquest. Was the product wrong, or have market conditions changed, or did the advertising agents do a bad job, or was the sales manager not after all the whiz-kid he or she had seemed to be? Any of these or similar explanations may be valid, of course. But it seems possible that the reason why marketing fails, or appears to fail, lies deeper than this.

The need for integration

The attitude which regards marketing as a bolt-on extra, of itself undermines any chance of success. Marketing cannot simply be added; it has to be integrated into the fabric of a company. The process is more analogous to weaving than to engineering. While marketing is viewed as something which can work by itself, there is little chance that it will work at all. When it is crossed with other threads that go to make the structure of a company, and in turn recrosses them time and time again, there is some hope that its main objectives will be secured.

So the relationship between marketing and other functions has to be examined. The way in which general managers, accountants, production managers and service chiefs see marketing can determine its success or failure, and their view is in turn influenced by the attitude of marketing people towards other departments. If we can look at these human factors in detail and find ways in which relations can be improved, we will have taken positive steps towards fully integrated marketing.

Subsequent chapters will therefore consider, department by department, the interaction between marketing and other important business functions. In each case the main problems likely to be met will be identified and some remedial measures discussed. Then the constituent parts of marketing itself, advertising, public relations, market research, the sales force and so on will be examined, to see how these relate to each other and to other departments of the company. It cannot be assumed that everything that might be included under the marketing umbrella is working to a common purpose, whatever organizational structure is in place.

Order of play

In adopting this approach the neat, compartmentalized format of marketing textbooks has to be abandoned. We shall be revisiting various departments and functions from time to time and looking at them from a different viewpoint, rather, I hope, as it happens at the place of work. At one moment, we may be discussing how a production manager might regard sales people, at another the attitude of sales representatives to the factory or to the product itself. By changing angles in this way it should be possible to get closer to the conditions under which business is actually conducted.

The problems of integration are human. They are not cured by any one specific technique, but by an understanding of the human factors involved in situations which are likely to occur. A number of first-hand examples have been given to illustrate those situations, and also some of the remedies I have attempted in the past, with varying degrees of success. After examining one department at a time in the course of Chapters 1 to 6, a comprehensive case study has been included which illustrates an authentic endeavour to integrate marketing effort in a tough and competitive field.

Then I have tried to draw the threads together and look at the basic steps a managing director might take towards integrating marketing, and at the sort of company in which it is most likely to flourish. Finally, a memorandum for decision takers has been included at the end of each chapter. This consists of some of the questions that might be raised in reference to your own company, and some of the action points that might be considered, should you feel that action is needed.

Verbal quibbles

Certain conventions have been used throughout for the sake of consistency. Where a department is referred to by a single word, such as Production, Development or Marketing, an initial capital letter has been employed to indicate that it is a *group of people* and not the function itself that is meant. Otherwise lower case letters have been used, so that the marketing department is written as such and not as the Marketing Department. This is simply to avoid peppering the book with capitals.

The people who do marketing are called marketors. They might equally well have been called marketeers or marketers. Both these expressions appear to have been coined in the USA before the word marketing was in common use on this side of the Atlantic. But even if we wished to follow American precedent a choice would still have to be made. I have chosen marketors partly in deference to the Worshipful Company of Marketors, but mostly because I prefer it to the alternatives.

It will be found that the central thesis of this book implies that marketing is a craft, and that it may be more fruitful to regard it as such, rather than as a profession. That could cause some heart-searching, so it may be as well at this point to give the main grounds for such an opinion, although the fullest explanation must lie in the chapters which follow.

Craft or profession?

If we consider the traditional image of a professional two aspects are relevant to business life. In the first place the professional owes allegiance to a code of practice which overrides any commercial affiliation. So a doctor, for example, should prescribe for the benefit of the patient, not to increase the profit of the practice or the hospital in which he or she happens to work. Even lawyers and accountants stand aloof from any organization to which they may belong when delivering professional judgements on how agreements are to be interpreted, or monetary transactions recorded.

As the purpose of this book is to seek ways of integrating marketing more closely – on the weaving analogy – a professional model that portrays the marketing manager as someone standing apart and offering advice on a 'take it or leave it' basis hardly seems appropriate. There are certainly standards of conduct to be observed, but it seems to be stretching a point to think of them as any other than those which govern honest business dealings, and decent relationships between individuals.

Then there is the question of qualification. In the past there has been a distinction, fostered by professionals, between the person who is qualified and one who merely aspires to be so. You were either qualified or not, and once you were, you were free to practise your profession. No one would be likely to view marketing qualifications in quite such black and white terms. Degrees and diplomas are evidence of study. Undoubtedly such study is worth while. It will have covered specific techniques and made familiar the concepts involved in marketing, and as a result the time taken to become an effective marketor should have been significantly shortened.

Nevertheless it is unlikely that anyone qualified in this way would immediately be put in charge of a sales team. Most companies would demand selling experience in the field as a precondition. Similarly with market research, advertising, product planning or any other aspect of marketing, some experience is normally required before full responsibility can be assumed. The best experience is of course that gained by working with a proven expert. So once more we are down to the analogy of craft skills. For me at any rate, marketing *feels* more like a craft than like a traditional profession.

It seems possible that in the future arguments about the definition of professionalism *vis-à-vis* craftsmanship will become increasingly pointless. Professionals themselves are seeing the wisdom of dismantling that part of professionalism that has been used as a barrier between them and the general public. It is not just that doctors, lawyers and others are having to take a more commercial view of life. They have perceived that to function more effectively they have to treat patients and clients as people. The fact that, however qualified you may be, it takes time to learn how to apply professional skills in human situations is now openly acknowledged.

There is common ground in this human dimension, which must narrow the gap between the ways in which professionals and craftsmen act, and impinge in turn on how they regard each other. So in practical terms the choice of a word to describe marketing activity may cease to matter. For me, and for the time being, it is more helpful to think of marketing as a craft with a number of facets to be mastered over time. As in other crafts what is produced is not right or wrong on some absolute scale; it either works with customers or it does not. And if it works it is either an elegant and appropriate solution to a problem, or something a little less than that. Like all good craftsmen, the marketor is always seeking a better way.

But if it is decided to call marketing a profession and if its status as such is accepted by all other departments, I shall not complain. What matters is that other parts of the company come to respect the marketing skills that are exercised in the common good, and that marketors ensure that this respect is mutual.

1

Red lamps, dry skin and cut corners

Limiting 'engineering attrition' in design and development

The most important item in the marketing mix is the product itself. Although this truth may from time to time be obscured in clouds of promotional hyperbole, it is immutable. Only the time-scale varies. It may take weeks, months or even years to become obvious, but eventually an attempt to sell a product which serves no useful purpose, or does its job badly, becomes desperately uphill work.

Unfortunately it is rare that the converse applies, and a first class product sells itself with no effort on our part. Nevertheless it remains the best sales aid imaginable. So it would seem logical to look at design and development first, to see how marketing can help to ensure that what finally emerges from the development process is right in every sense.

At this point a well-trained marketing theorist might raise objections, both to my batting order and to the language used.

> What do you mean, development comes first? Surely market research comes first, to find out what is wanted. And why do you say *help* to ensure? Isn't marketing's job to tell the designers what is required of them? Aren't you adopting far too low a profile?

I hope to answer these questions in the course of this chapter, and to suggest a role for marketing which is appropriate to the way in which products actually come into being.

Market research and new products

To clear the ground it may be as well to consider market research in relation to product development. It should be, and indeed is, possible to ask potential customers what they want. The difficulty lies in obtaining meaningful answers. Of course if the product already exists and what is sought is some improvement, or something similar to, but competitive with, another company's offering, it may be helpful to ask questions of existing users. We can even ask non-users what has inhibited them from buying. There are however two main problems, even in such straightforward circumstances.

In the first place users tend to look at what they have, not what they might have instead of it. If there are major limitations in a product these will be revealed in the research, but were probably common knowledge anyway. Mostly the improvements suggested are minor, because customers have come to accept what has been purchased on its own terms. So it is rare that market research produces any radical suggestions for a new product. If an improved version is all that is required, it may be as well to conduct a survey as a means of checking that your ideas, or those of your engineers, are in line with your customers' thinking. Even this usefulness may however be limited if development is going to take time and competitors are actively working on improvements of their own. By the time your product emerges it might have to face different standards of comparison.

The second difficulty in research prior to design and development is in the question of an acceptable price. Many customers would be willing to accept more features for no extra cost, and all would like to pay less for what is already available, but how much they would be willing to pay for real improvements, and what market price levels will be by the time of the launch, are not easy matters to ascertain.

Engineering-led development

Do we then just give the engineers their head, and reserve our research and our comments until their efforts produce something concrete? An examination of products launched over the years would seem to indicate that it is engineering, not marketing, which has set the pace. The Industrial Revolution harnessed new sources of power and enabled metals to be worked in ways previously unimagined. Perfectly viable and economical canals were, in the space of a few years, abandoned for railways. The engineers were in the lead and the rest of the world followed.

Something similar has happened in the technological revolution still in progress. The principle seems to have been: 'if it can be done, it should be done.' Electronic devices with an ever-larger capacity have resulted in machines being designed with a multiplicity of functions. Long lists of these adorn the advertisements of rival manufacturers. The bewildered user, who may only want to perform quite simple tasks efficiently, is urged to buy the latest 'future-proof' equipment. His or her ideas of what is good or not-so-good in electronics are being manufactured along with the hardware. And although some earlier excesses have failed the test of usage, and equipment is appearing which is both cheaper and easier to operate, what is or is not 'user-friendly' is still largely defined by electronics experts rather than their customers.

Although at times of rapid change engineering-led design may be inevitable, it is nevertheless something which should always prompt a marketor to think twice. Some checks and balances are needed, if only because there seems no reason to believe, and several grounds for doubt, that engineers are typical of the people for whom they are designing things.

Red lamps

Take, for instance, the display panels that are a feature of so many machines of different kinds. For years the letters and numbers appearing on these were shown in red. In some cases this is still the practice. Yet red is not the easiest colour to see, especially if sunlight happens to fall on the panel. The operators of machines are often men, and men, more so than women, are prone to varying degrees of colour blindness. For me red is a dull colour and hard to see until I am really close to whatever is emitting red light. Engineers seem immune to this common human weakness. Whenever I asked our development department why some other colour could not have been chosen, the reply was that red was more easily obtainable, and what was the problem anyway?

It seems unfair to blame their myopia rather than my colour blindness. After all they were participating in a long and honourable tradition. Ships at sea show red lights to port and green to starboard. No one seems ever to have suggested that yellow or violet might be superior. On the contrary, would-be navigating officers are tested for colour vision and rejected if they cannot discern the dim reds or greens with which they are confronted. After that there is, naturally, no problem.

Happily in the case of display panels someone saw the advantage of producing them in colours that might be as visible to men as to women so a wider variety became available. This advance is now in turn threatened by the increasing use that is being made of what are called 'liquid crystal' displays. These use less current but are again quite difficult to see in sunlight. Once more it is the engineers, not the users, who set the fashion.

Even when marketing does have a voice in matters of this sort, it may have to be an emphatic voice to make any impression. Two personal, and in themselves quite minor, anecdotes may serve to illustrate this.

Dry skin

One classic way of overcoming a weakness is to treat it as a strength. As marketing director of a 'high tech' business I saw no possibility of matching the detailed knowledge of our own engineers and technicians, yet I was not willing to accept without question their opinions of what was or was not right for our customers. So I took a deep interest in anything new and insisted on handling it and using it as a customer might, before committing us to selling it.

One product to come under consideration was a bedside radio and communication system for hotels. The new bedhead unit was proudly shown to me: elegant, with a row of buttons of the type often used in lifts, but smaller. These 'buttons' have no moving parts but respond to a finger laid on them, which makes a change to their electrical condition. They are neat, safe and in our case offered advantages in reliability and ease of maintenance over anything yet seen in hotel room systems. There was just one problem: when I put my finger on them they either failed to work or worked incorrectly. The response from the development team was one of shocked amazement. After a pause for thought and some consultation among themselves they came up with the answer: 'We believe we know what is wrong with you – you have dry skin!'

By now I was used to acknowledging my faults: first colour blindness and then dry skin. But I did point out that, should a significant proportion of hotel guests also have dry skin, the consequences for us could be quite expensive. Sadly we reverted to the older type of button.

Cut corners

Before we look at more systematic ways of handling this type of problem, a further example may help to indicate the nature of the difficulties involved, and the human factors which need to be incorporated into any workable solution. In this case there was really no need for design or development. All that was required was a thorough technical evaluation. The product was a time-clock of the kind used in factories to stamp the cards of workers entering or leaving. We had a gap in our range but found an excellent machine manufactured in Germany, for which we could obtain the distributorship.

A number were sent over for evaluation and one was installed in my office, so that, for a month of so, I could clock in or clock out whenever I went through the door. The clock cards used by the Germans had rounded corners and were quite expensive. We had always used cards with squared corners and had our local source of supply. For this evaluation I was using our cards, cut to the correct size for the machine.

After a time I found that the machine developed a habit of swallowing cards, so that they were put in for stamping but failed to emerge. I borrowed a screwdriver to investigate and began to suspect the channels of the feed mechanism. A full technical examination confirmed this. The squaring of the cards enabled them to escape from the grooves designed to hold them. There was no problem at all with the rounded corners used by the Germans. This time nobody blamed me. The question that had to be asked was why no one had talked to the manufacturers about their reasons for using rounded cards. The real answer lay in the natural desire of our own people to go one better, to use our own cheaper cards and so to score points over the Germans.

Here it might be thought, by anyone unkind enough to do so, that my particular engineers were not merely parochial, but downright incompetent. If so, they were in good company. Far better qualified people have made bigger and more public mistakes. Buildings which develop structural faults and have to be pulled down, missile systems which prove incapable of hitting low flying aircraft, early warning radar which cannot recognize objects on the ground: there are many major projects which reach an advanced and costly stage before they are aborted. Instances such as these have received the enthusiastic attention of the press in the past and will do so again. Our own engineers were no more prone to mistakes than others working on new products. The issue is not one of eliminating human error, but of recognizing what is likely to happen in development, and ensuring that marketing makes whatever contribution it can to producing something that customers will want to buy.

The examples given, though in themselves very simple, will have pointed up the dangers of engineering-led design, and indicated one route that might be taken to draw the efforts of marketing people and development engineers closer together. If it is considered a highly personal approach, depending for its success on the relationships between the individuals engaged in each form of activity, there are grounds for believing that, in the ultimate, it is relationships of this kind that make or break a company's new product programme. No quantities of paperwork, screening processes or formal procedures of any kind are anywhere near so important. Nevertheless there is a need to establish some sort of framework within which these relationships can flourish, and there may be stages in this where a clear understanding of who is in the driving seat may be required.

Alternative approaches

Two extremes should be considered, although the most fruitful approach could lie in some combination of the two, however discrepant they may appear to be. One line of thought suggests a more 'commercial' relationship between departments. In this case Marketing in effect 'buys' the product from Development, before selling it on to its own customers. By *distancing* development in this way it is hoped that a more effective discipline will prevail on all sides. Marketing will have to say clearly what it wants and how much it will pay for it. Development will then have to say exactly what it is offering and when it will be available. Differences of view will be dealt with at the outset, and Marketing will have the right to accept or reject the final product, should it not match the original specification.

The apparent advantage of this approach is that it avoids the vagueness and compromise which can accompany less formal methods. It brings clarity to a process which otherwise results all too often in unpleasant surprises and disappointments: 'But this is not what we wanted!' or 'How on earth can we sell it if it costs that much?' By distancing development activity the process of creating a new product becomes, from the marketing point of view, more like that of buying an item from an external source for subsequent resale.

The distancing approach finds a natural home in large companies with separate research establishments. Yet it is possible to feel that such organizations are not noticeably better at innovation than smaller firms. There are indeed some difficulties in conducting development on an 'arm's length' basis, which will become apparent as we go through the stages involved in the process.

Before doing this a brief look should be taken at the alternative approach: *involvement*. Here the marketing influence is present throughout, so that what emerges should have been agreed stage by stage from the beginning, with little risk of rejection at the end. There are advantages in this method too, not the least being a cross-fertilization of ideas as the project proceeds. At its best involvement should keep engineers aware of real customer needs, and enable marketors to frame their requirements in the light of the soundest predictions of technical advances.

In practice involvement can easily result in botched compromises which have more to do with office politics than with interdepartmental brainstorming. Distancing however can produce a similar level of mediocrity. This is because in a strictly formal and more commercial regime, caution is likely to prevail over imagination, so that Marketing will never share the more speculative ideas generated within the development department.

What seems to work best is a system which blends elements from each approach. The exact mixture may vary with the personalities involved, and perhaps from project to project. Nevertheless, there are fixed points in the process which are common to all development activity. These have to be considered in greater detail.

Product specification

Unless we are going to accept engineering-led design in its entirety, Marketing has to begin the development process with a clear statement of the sort of product it wants. Even if the original idea for something new came from someone in Engineering, Marketing has to define its shape and size, its features, how it compares with competitive products, what it offers its customers and what it should cost, all in terms of the market into which it will be sold. This stage therefore seems well suited to a distancing approach. Marketing says what is needed; the development department says whether such a project is feasible, how long it will take and what the development costs will be.

In practice this neat and logical division of labour seems quite difficult to realize. Attempts to make it a formal procedure for all projects, large or small, seem to dampen enthusiasm for new ideas, or to produce paperwork that reflects less a statement of a market requirement than a political compromise. This of course is exactly what distancing is supposed to avoid. What seems to happen is that, when put to the test, marketing people find it quite hard to draw up a specification that is both right for the market and has a reasonable chance of coming to fruition.

It would naturally be easy enough to specify a product with all the features any customer has ever requested, at a lower cost than any competitive offering. But it might not be so easy to make one. Even if it were accomplished, should development take a year or two, by the time the product emerged it might no longer have so clear a lead. So a really aggressive, or optimistic, marketor should perhaps add an impossible time-scale to an over-ambitious set of physical parameters. Most marketing managers however have no wish to alienate their colleagues and are too sensitive to the realities of life to make demands of this sort.

Nevertheless what is or is not over-ambitious is a matter of opinion. In avoiding one pitfall it is easy to swing too far the other way and produce a specification not of what the market requires but of what is believed to be within the technical competence of the company. If a pessimistic view is taken of this, sights may be set too low at the outset and the resultant product is unlikely to please anyone.

To avoid either extreme, knowledge of the market needs to be blended with an objective view of what is technically possible, whether or not the company has yet employed the relevant technology. This would seem to imply that some dialogue with engineers is needed, to frame a specification which is either feasible or capable of being tested for feasibility without excessive expense. A raw, distancing approach is often quite inadequate in such circumstances. The judgements that have to be made by Marketing in drawing up a specification can be too complex for that.

It is sometimes hard enough to see what customers will want in two or three years' time, and how much they might then be prepared to pay for it, regardless of technical limitations. To form a view it may be necessary to look beyond the opinions users hold of current products and examine the fundamental tasks those products are performing, to assess just how attractive a different or cheaper method might be. When it is not known for sure whether such a product is possible within the time-scale, because, for example, product cost might depend heavily on the purchase of a new microchip not now available and as yet unpriced, someone just has to talk to competent engineers before a full market specification can be created.

Yet in spite of the need for dialogue in its formative stages, the specification itself must represent a commitment by Marketing to the product it wishes to see made. And however much has been contributed by engineers in predicting the technological climate or in commenting on the feasibility of various options, what is being specified has to be what the market will in future need, not what would be easiest to make.

The language in which a specification is written should reflect this. As far as possible it should be written in plain language rather than in 'engineer speak'. Of course if there are official standards which have to be met, reference will be made to them. Some products are technical in their nature: chemicals, for example, or materials and components to be used by customers in their own manufacturing processes. The determining factor is the same however in all cases. It is the language used by customers to describe the features they require. This, rather than in-company jargon should be the starting point for a new product. It brings the customer closer to the engineer. It also avoids any suggestion that, in using technical terms, marketing people are trying to teach engineers their job.

A further means of producing an acceptable and viable specification may be to divide the parameters stated into those that are:

- necessary
- desirable.

It would be rare to find all features of equal importance in the market place and a measure of flexibility may help to produce an acceptable outcome and to save time. If such a distinction is made, Marketing may want to lay down separate cost limits for products with different degrees of sophistication.

Once a written specification has been issued and accepted it forms something like an internal contract between Marketing and Development. Afterwards the agreed brief should not be altered by either side without serious consultation. To this extent a degree of formality at the initial stages may help to prevent misunderstandings later. But the process that creates a good brief is, as we have seen, far removed from an arm's length, distant approach. And if an internal contract is implied, it is as well to remember that the most successful contracts are between people who hold each other in mutual esteem.

We have now to look carefully at what happens as development proceeds. The main responsibility has been placed firmly within the orbit of Engineering. The question is whether Marketing has any role to play until a product is placed before it to receive a ritual blessing. The examples given earlier will have betrayed my own view all too well. As a marketing director I took a deep interest in the progress of development. In turn our engineers were happy to use me as a sounding board for the various ideas they needed to try out. Of itself, this merely reflects the personal relationships that existed in a particular company at one time. It hardly constitutes a method of operation. It was however part of a system of defences we had erected against the dangers of engineering attrition.

Engineering attrition

This is a phenomenon which, in the absence of any precautions against it, would appear inevitable. It is the rule which ensures that the product which finally emerges either does less or costs more than was originally promised, or, quite likely, does less *and* costs more.

It is naturally most easy to observe in large projects, such as the Channel Tunnel, where 'and takes longer' could be added to the list of shortcomings. In cases such as this the very complexity of the project makes problems more likely, although it could be argued that large undertakings attract large management resources to keep them in line. But engineering attrition is a hazard of all new developments, large or small. Somehow, by a series of steps almost imperceptible at the time, the finished version comes to do a little less than expected, however simple and straightforward it appeared to be.

Perhaps it is not entirely fair to call the phenomenon 'engineering' attrition. In some cases Marketing will revise forecasts downwards, so that it suddenly costs more to buy in components in smaller quantities. Sometimes suppliers will cease to exist, or raise prices against expectation. Even simple developments, however, provide ample scope for calculations to be revised, longer time allowed, new testing procedures found to be essential or more expensive materials demanded. Engineers have at their disposal a hundred and one ways of making modifications to the original specification seem reasonable and unavoidable. So how is this menace to be controlled?

Communication

The involvement indicated in the examples quoted points towards a need for communication throughout the whole process of creating and evaluating new products. The snag is that communication can be a means of undermining the original conception, so that what was specified quite clearly is gradually eroded in a series of conversations between individuals or in meetings where the implications of any suggested amendment are not fully explored. Each amendment may be minor in itself but the cumulative effect of a number of them could be serious. This is exactly how the more refined forms of engineering attrition operate. So involvement and interest have to function within certain established ground rules, if they are not to be self-defeating.

One of these is that any proposed change, however small, should be recorded and circulated to all concerned. In an open company a reading file could be established containing any and all references to the project, from whatever source. Marketing is then in a position to respond to anything which appears to affect the specification, and to ask questions if in doubt. Equally, any change in the market foreseen for the product, or in sales forecasts will be known to Development. Such a system is not proof against hidden agendas, but it should eliminate inadvertent misunderstandings.

Marketing involvement is better directed to the end result rather than to the precise means of getting there. There are many occasions when an engineer will have an idea, but will not be quite sure whether it will work. He or she may well wish to conduct a few experiments in the laboratory before discussing it with anyone. Involvement does not mean standing behind someone's shoulder or making bright suggestions on engineering matters. Generally engineers are best left to do their job, and trusted to speak up if there is anything that should be said. The existence of a product specification serves to highlight factors of importance to the success of the project. If, for example, any 'necessary' feature appears to be in peril, the problem should be disclosed immediately.

Apart from the discipline imposed by an agreed specification, and good communication throughout development, the most effective ways of curbing engineering attrition come towards the end of the process. Their value is not simply that Marketing has a right of refusal, as a commercial approach to development would imply. It is that the knowledge that the product will be tested in the market place before being launched helps to focus everyone's attention on the needs of the customer rather than on more domestic issues. The principal means to this end are market acceptance tests and field trials.

Market acceptance tests

Once I had a colleague who designed a new shape of telephone. He was confident it would be welcomed by our customers. All those in Marketing who had seen it were enthusiastic. It had cost a good deal of money to develop but the result appeared attractive. There was pressure to launch it as soon as possible. Nevertheless our routine included a test of acceptability in the market-place, which most people thought would be a formality.

We had models made which were included in a case with other instruments available on the market at the time. All were the same colour, to ensure as far as possible that we were testing reaction to shape alone. They were shown to a number of people at different levels in companies which would be likely to buy equipment of that type. To our surprise the majority, including both decision makers and those who might influence decisions, preferred the existing shapes to the new one. The margin was such that no amount of sales promotion would be likely to bridge the gap.

Naturally my colleague was disturbed by the results of our survey, and even more so by my subsequent rejection of the instrument. From the development team came howls of anguish: 'But you were all as enthusiastic as we were! What about all the money invested in this project? Are you saying we should now drop it, and recover nothing?' That, of course, apart from natural human disappointment, was exactly the issue. Money had been spent, and had to be recovered. But the cost of abortive development can only be regained from profits. In this instance we could make more profit, faster, by continuing to sell existing shapes than by attempting to launch the new one.

Acceptance tests can take many forms, some far less structured than the example given here. The more casual approach adopted in our case study in Chapter 7 produced quite valid results. The point is that some attempt should be made to step outside the euphoria which can attend the completion of a development project and to take an objective look at what we now have to offer and at the likely reaction of potential customers. At the other extreme are the elaborate test-marketing exercises staged by consumer companies, where a new product is offered for sale, but only in selected areas. These can test much more than customers' reaction to the product as such, and further research may be needed to isolate responses to the product from other factors involved in its promotion and in the decision to buy.

Field trials

Some things demand more than an instant customer response to prove their viability. With machinery in particular there seems to be a rule that no engineer in the laboratory can make it go wrong as easily as an operator in the field. This may be because laboratory tests just cannot simulate the wide variety of conditions under which a product will be used, or perhaps because its creator handles a product with knowledge and care, while a purchaser may be more clumsy, and not show quite the same concern.

Examples are plentiful. Take the first automatic cash dispensers to be installed in the walls of banks. Serious problems were found with overheating. Perhaps no one told the development engineers where and how the machines were going to be used. In any event the banks simply took them, built them into their solid outer walls, and let the public discover what was wrong. Then there was the advanced passenger train. It should have been possible to try this out on a random collection of 'passengers', representing a fair sample of the general population, before discovering at the public launch that it made travellers seasick on bends in the track.

Field trials are designed to identify problems of this kind before a product is put on sale. They take longer than market acceptance tests because it is not the immediate appeal of the project which is under scrutiny, but its working in normal operating conditions. The fact that such trials appear sometimes to have been omitted is significant. There may be purely physical reasons for this. Some products are so large and so prominent that a discreet trial is quite impossible. But even small products with a wide range of potential customers are often launched without preliminary trials.

The main reason for this is the psychological pressure that has been building during the development process. So much effort and enthusiasm has gone into the product that no one wants to delay its launch. It has passed all its laboratory tests and matches the marketing brief exactly. No one can foresee any problems. But field trials are not designed to catch problems that have been foreseen. They are intended to identify and overcome the unforeseen difficulties that have ruined the launch of many an otherwise acceptable product.

The marketing department may feel frustration at this stage, just as much as the development engineers. This is all the more likely if the new product is designed to replace an existing one and stocks are running low, or if competitors are known to be on the point of launching their own, updated versions of the product. But the marketing task at this time is to look for typical but quite obscure customers, preferably situated within reasonable distance of the laboratory, and persuade them to try the equipment, before any public announcements are made.

A marketing veto

Both market acceptance tests and field trials imply some sort of marketing veto over a product which has been developed to an agreed specification, and perhaps with the close involvement of marketing people at all subsequent stages. This is the ultimate sanction and its existence should ensure that marketing's influence on development is real enough. The justification for such a veto is that it costs far less than the veto that might be applied by the public after an expensive and abortive launch. If it is an accepted part of the company's procedures for handling new products, it is unlikely to be used very often.

If it ever has to be invoked there will naturally be some heart-searching, not the least on the part of the chief executive. The competence of Development to design a product and of Marketing to sell it will be equally open to question. It is then that underlying attitudes are vital to a quick recovery. If mutual respect exists between departments and their respective roles are thoroughly understood, what will then be discussed is not who is to blame but what the next project will be.

Questions and action points for decision takers

Does development start with a written product specification?

Who creates this?

What advice is available on technological trends?

Is the specification written in language that customers could understand?

Has any distinction been made between necessary and desirable features?

Have cost limits been set accordingly?

How are any amendments communicated to and from everybody concerned?

What market acceptance tests are planned?

Who will conduct them?

What arrangements have been made for field trials before a public launch?

Has Marketing found suitable customers for these trials?

Is it understood that Marketing will reject the product if it falls short of expectation?

2

Crossing the blue–white divide

Relations with production, installation and service departments

Industry is about making things. This is self-evident to workers on the shop-floor, to their immediate bosses, and to the public at large. It is only marketors who think otherwise, and perhaps accountants who might, in their turn, consider industry to be about making money. So marketors, with their minds full of sophisticated ways and means of matching customers' needs to the capabilities of their company, would do well to contemplate the high probability of a completely different set of attitudes prevailing elsewhere in the organization.

Perhaps it is a sign of progress that such differences are now perceptible. Not so very long ago entire companies were oriented towards production. Even their marketing staff, or those with the words 'marketing' or 'sales' on their visiting cards, thought that way. When I was first finding my feet as a new sales manager in a subsidiary company of GEC I was summoned to headquarters for a meeting at which sales executives of various units would make presentations. The worthy objective was to let each other know what was on offer across the group as a whole. It was an important occasion at which the chief himself would be present, and gave an opportunity, I thought, for bright young marketors to shine.

After a brief preamble we took it in turn around the table to explain our businesses. The first speakers dropped into a uniform format on the lines of:

> We have two factories, one in Liverpool and the other in Slough. In Liverpool we make product X and in Slough product Y ....

It was all clear and factual so long as you knew what product X and product Y were for, and who used them – which I, for one, did not.

I had however anticipated such an approach and had determined to tackle the job from the other end, starting with our customers. When it was my turn, armed with some simple visual aids, I prepared to give an account of the markets we served and how we sold to them. But, as luck would have it, no sooner had I got to my feet than the chief was called away to an international telephone call, and I was left speaking in an apparent void to a vaguely hostile audience. So are reputations made and lost. When the chief returned everyone brightened up and proceeded happily to the next exposition of factory locations and the next list of products made there.

Of course GEC and most of industry has moved on since then. Greater use is now made of the word 'marketing', and sometimes it is more than just a longer word for 'sales'. It would however be a mistake to assume that the concept as it now stands is understood and appreciated in all departments. There are good reasons why this is unlikely to be the case, especially in the factory itself.

Spatial separation

The worker in the factory is often spatially and culturally remote from people in the marketing department. Both aspects of this have important consequences. Cultural perceptions and social barriers, real or imagined, have received a good deal of attention from industrial psychologists, but the impact of geographical separation may be quite as severe, and at the very least serves to reinforce feelings of isolation.

It is inevitable that there will be some distance between people sitting at desks studying sales graphs and people working at noisy and often messy manufacturing processes. Sometimes this is a few metres only, say to an office block on the same site. Even that is enough to differentiate workers on the shop-floor from 'them upstairs'. Often the distance is much greater. Governments and regional authorities have in the past offered companies incentives to spread their production facilities up and down the entire length of the country. The financial benefits have appeared indisputable and the ensuing communication problems easily surmountable by better use of data links and high-technology telephone systems. Naturally these help, but attitudes are seldom shaped over the telephone, except for the worse. There is no substitute for face to face human contact, and the price of ignoring this is paid in instalments, some small and some very large indeed, and few ever attributed to the underlying cause.

At a time of rapid expansion for a company of which I was then marketing director, I experienced some of the dilemmas that even a mild form of spatial separation can bring. We had a site on an industrial estate which had been purchased with an eye to growth. There was spare land beyond the car park on which on 5 November each year we held fireworks parties. These were popular with employees in all departments and with their families. The land had no other use.

In spite of this, when the need for additional office space became pressing, strong arguments were put forward against extending our building on the site already owned. There was a high capital cost, and how sure were we that expansion would continue? Besides this, the administration manager had found another building on the same industrial estate that would shortly become vacant. It was just the right size and was available at a low rental. The only problem was that the car park was too small for both staff and visitors.

There was no way in which my unquantifiable doubts could prevail against the case made. After all, the lease was short term and we still had the option of building at a later date. The risks appeared minimal. Yet there were indications of problems to come, even before the lease was signed. The administration manager proposed to call the new building Unit B. This struck me as unwise, since it would be bound to imply an alphabetical superiority for those housed in Unit A. I took a compass to the site, lined up the buildings and decided that, give or take 18 degrees, one location would be called North Building and the other one South Building. That represented a small victory in the struggle against bureaucracy, but heavier engagements were looming. Because they were the fastest growing, a number of my departments were scheduled to move to 'Unit B ... sorry, North Building'. The question was, should I move with them?

Here was a nasty decision. If I stayed behind the departments moving could well feel a sense of neglect, as if they were somehow in exile, and removed from the centre of decision-making. On the other hand, the rest of my troops were staying put, as were the other directors of the company, including the managing director. If I moved there was a chance that I would be the one to suffer isolation, and that in consequence the company would drift into a state of schism, if not civil war.

In the end I stayed behind. The price of doing so for me was innumerable walks across the industrial estate in an attempt to do my job in two places at the same time. At least it was healthy exercise. For others I suspect the price was higher. In spite of all our efforts the company never regained the sense of unity it had previously enjoyed. It may be more than coincidence that there were no more fireworks parties on the ground that had been left free.

This is a minor example of the effects of spatial separation. Its significance is that there were no solid grounds for anticipating a problem. It involved only a stone's throw move on the part of a number of people all doing head office, administrative jobs of one kind or another. The work performed in either the North or the South Building would have seemed to an outside observer to have been of a broadly similar nature. When we are considering a more radical split, between, say, Manufacturing and all other departments, including Marketing, or greater geographical distances between departments, the consequences can be much more severe. Furthermore, if the situation has existed for long enough any adverse results may well be attributed to other causes, organizational or personal, while the geographical position is regarded merely as the board on which management games are played.

Cultural distinctions

To this common cause of differences in attitude we have to add the cultural factors which are typified in the distinction between blue and white collar workers. It is not surprising that Japanese companies in particular are making great efforts to eliminate broad distinctions of this kind, at least within the manufacturing plant itself. It is likely that some of the more extreme manifestations of the blue–white divide will be eroded over the new few years. Obvious targets are management dining rooms, weekly pay envelopes and differences in dress. But attitudes built up over the years are not changed easily. Management and workers alike have moved on from their film caricatures in Charlie Chaplin's *Modern Times*, and from those of a generation later portrayed in *I'm All Right, Jack*, with Peter Sellers as the archetypal shop steward. The tendency to think in terms of 'them' and 'us' is however sustained by the very facts of production life. The conditions under which things are made must often differ from those under which the same articles are sold, so differences of outlook are going to persist.

The factory worker sees materials and subassemblies coming in and finished goods going to the dispatch bay. There may in some cases be a sense of the wide world beyond derived from the labels on consignments headed for exotic locations, but in general all thought and action is concentrated between the entry and exit points of the works premises. So any job satisfaction is likely to be present there, too, or not exist at all.

Job satisfaction is a notoriously difficult thing to pin down, clear of all hypocrisy or special pleading. What satisfies one person may have no relevance to another. Yet it must be the case that any satisfaction experienced must fall within the bounds of the job itself, in its broadest sense. So people who make things are not likely to be motivated by factors which appeal to people who sell things, especially when these two forms of activity are kept separate and performed in different places. Marketors have sometimes failed to appreciate this. The integration of marketing and manufacturing effort is never likely to be easy, or a matter of a few well-chosen words.

Two personal examples may serve to point up the different attitudes that may exist within the factory, and how far removed they may be from those of salesmen and saleswomen. I once knew a woman who looked back wistfully on her days as a factory hand. Her job had been putting almonds on cakes as they came by on a conveyor belt. Now this sounded rather dull, even a little reminiscent of *Modern Times*. Yet no job afterwards had been, to quote her: 'as interesting'. The reason was that her fingers could work happily on the cakes while she chatted with the other women working on the line. She liked them and they liked her. It was one, day-long, social occasion.

Then in the south of France I talked to the manager of a factory where complicated switches were made. He had a traditional assembly line, where each worker added a piece to the switch until it was complete. He also had some 'work stations' at which a young woman sitting at a semi-circular bench, built the switch completely herself. The theory was, of course, that this latter method would appeal more to the operator and produce better results. When I asked which had proved the better way in practice, he replied that in terms of cost and quality there was little to choose between them, while as far as job satisfaction was concerned, some employees liked one method and some the other. He considered that by allowing the choice he got the best of both worlds. Some workers were proud of assembling the complete switch themselves, others were happier with a single, repetitive operation at which they had become adept: just as if they were putting almonds on cakes.

Naturally there is a great deal more that has been and could be said about shop-floor motivation. The examples given here have stayed in my mind, because they were so different from the textbook image of what constitutes job satisfaction, especially where go-getting young marketors are concerned. They do not cover more than a fraction of the range of motivation to be found within a factory, but they may indicate once again that it is inside the factory that any motivation which exists will be found. It is not something that can be imported from outside.

Perceived threats

Where there is likely to be unanimity in the workshop is in the reaction to anything seen as a threat. The marketor might see this as an opportunity to inject some of his or her own customer-oriented attitudes into the manufacturing unit. The threats seen by Marketing are often real enough. They stem from the activities of competitors or from factors which may depress the market as a whole. But threats of this kind can appear very remote from the shop-floor. We will look later at ways of bridging that gap. For the moment it is as well to appreciate that the factory may see the marketing department itself as a threat.

The task of production is made much easier if orders for identical amounts are received on a regular basis. In a workers' paradise this would be the natural state of things. But of course there is a serpent in the garden, and its name is Marketing. Marketing creates surges in demand which are hard to accommodate, and Marketing is responsible for falling order levels which promote fears of redundancy. Marketing is, or should be, striving for change, while for many people in the workshop change is uncomfortable. Its activities may therefore be a focus for those defensive attitudes which are latent in the factory.

Even without stimulation the nature of the production process often lends itself to defensive practices which ultimately have an impact in the market-place. Take, for example, the case of a company which allocates costs to individual jobs or projects. No worker likes logging 'idle time', so when there is a hitch for any reason, the minutes and hours wasted tend to get allocated to some job or other. The choice may well fall on an unpopular project, or one that is large and on-going, that is, a 'dustbin' job to which a few hours can be added without raising any awkward queries. If this distortion is not noticed the result is passed through to the invoicing department and thence to the customer. In minor instances this may cause no more than a raised eyebrow, but the next time an order is placed it may go elsewhere. So matters of business may be determined by choices made on the shop floor.

Real problems

Good production managers deplore such practices just as much as the sales representative who finds the price inflated by excessive labour costs or the estimator trying to understand what has gone wrong. Production managers however have a difficult job to do. Even if they had only to make 500 a week of a perfectly standard product, they would still have problems with supplies, sickness, holidays, the recruitment and training of the right people, personal conflicts, over-zealous union officials, the Health and Safety inspector and quality control. Furthermore, they too would undoubtedly prefer a steady order rate, few product changes, a limited range of shapes and sizes and quality standards set by engineers to tolerances which made some allowance for less-than-perfect work. And here is a marketing manager, faced with none of the problems that beset Production, demanding more rapid delivery, requesting 'specials', querying costs and insisting that quality has to be improved to meet competition.

Causes of conflict

The essence of this situation is that both manufacturers and marketors consider themselves to be 'at the sharp end' of the business. From here the path downwards is all too clear. Geographical remoteness may serve to widen a functional and cultural gap, so that the real enemy becomes not a competitor but another department of the same company. Production managers and marketing managers alike may feel a greater sense of kinship with their counterparts in competitive companies than with the strangers they meet across the table in their own firm's conference room.

It is important to appreciate that the potential for this sort of mayhem is always present on both sides. We have been looking hard at Production, because of the need for marketors to understand what may be going on in the minds of factory workers and their immediate bosses. Many conflicts however have their origins on the marketing side, perhaps through a lack of such understanding. The sales representative who insists that everything else is dropped in favour of a particular customer, or who promises a quite unrealistic delivery date to obtain an order, is highly likely to produce a clash of interest, which if repeated often enough becomes a running battle.

If Marketing is to be fully effective conflicts with Production have to be reduced to an absolute minimum. Practical methods for achieving this need to be examined. It is unlikely that there is any one golden key to a fully integrated approach to customers, but a number of quite modest steps, taken together, can change the atmosphere in which people work. A test of success will be when no one talks any more of 'cooperation' between Manufacturing and Marketing. Use of that word is a sure indication of underlying conflict. Exhortation to greater cooperation, or indeed exhortation of any kind, is better left to politicians. So let us look at what can be done.

The role of the product manager

In larger companies a key part can be played by a product manager. The definition of this function and exact terms of reference will vary from one company to another, and may be combined with other responsibilities. Duties that are relevant to our discussion lie in the general area of marketing planning and include:

- ensuring that the product is right for its intended market
- seeing that it is priced correctly
- forecasting sales
- controlling the range of products offered
- establishing the delivery times that may be quoted.

As such the function is distinct from sales promotion or from selling, although in a small company the same person might handle them as well. The distinction is important because a product manager has to think globally about the product range. It may, for example, be necessary to weigh the advantages of accepting an order requiring special modifications to the product against the disruption to normal output that this would cause. To make sensible judgements on such matters he or she will need to act in close liaison with the manufacturing manager, and would benefit from being completely at home in the factory itself. Once someone is in this position the sales function also has to be modified. For the job of the sales department is then to obtain not just orders but orders within the parameters set up by the product manager.

Such an appointment paves the way for better relations between Marketing and Production. It may also push some of the potential conflicts back into the marketing department, but they are better handled there, since the product manager is after all a marketor and should be equipped to handle them. Where the interface with Production is concerned opportunities for achieving a better understanding lie in a wise use of market research, in an analysis of product profitability, in sales forecasting and in the exercise of delivery discipline as well as in control of the product range. These areas are closely related to activities already taking place in the factory, for example the ordering of materials, production scheduling and quality control. So the establishment of the product management function can bring quick results. The reorganization it entails can however be a delicate matter. This is because the responsibilities listed will, in however rudimentary a form, be considered to lie within someone else's sphere of influence already. Any change will have to be explained with care, and positive results demonstrated without delay. If the first fruits of the new appointment are seen as a flood of forms to be completed by other departments, you have either appointed the wrong person, or given the wrong briefing.

Market research

The limitations of market research when seeking ideas for new products have already been noted in Chapter 1. No such limitations are present if all we want to do is to check the status of existing products or services offered by the company. How our products are rated by users and non-users, what competitors are recognized and how they are ranked, what features are considered important, how prices compare, what delivery time is expected: these and other factors of interest can often be revealed by a well-designed but simple survey.

The advantage of having objective information on such points is great. Until the questions have been asked and the replies analysed, all anyone has as a basis for action is opinion. The factory may believe it is turning out the right product at the right cost. A sales representative, sent packing by the last customer seen, may think that competition has the edge in features or quality or price. The scope for argument and disagreement is wide. With good market research arguments may be settled in a way that is as acceptable to Production as it is to the sales department. It is as if the customer, or a sample of customers, has been brought face to face with the manufacturer.

Naturally for this to be effective communication has to be both open and comprehensive. Production has to know exactly what is going on, and a full account must be given of the methods employed in the research programme. Presentation of results is critical. If an outside agency is used care must be taken to ensure that its results are presented by someone who understands the business, not by a researcher unaware of the implications of the data obtained, or unable to give a clear indication of the degree of credence that can be given to individual findings.

Straightforward industrial surveys, of the type briefly described here, are comparatively quick and comparatively inexpensive. They are, however, likely to take a few weeks. To this must be added the time that will be needed for a newly appointed product manager to learn to recognize the really important questions to which answers must be sought. As a result market research, although one of the most potent ways of bringing Production and Marketing together, is unlikely to yield the fast return we are seeking from the appointment of a product manager. There are other routes to this, which use information already available or at least information that can be extracted from what is available.

Forecasting sales

Every manufacturing unit will need to forecast its output in both the long and the short term. Within the factory there will be records of past production, which can be extrapolated into the future. The output achieved in the past is however a poor guide to what will be demanded in the weeks or months to come. It may have been inflated by the 'catching up' process that follows a period of shortages or delays. It may be sensitive to the mix of products involved which could be different in future. At best it gives some guide to the capacity of the plant to produce a given volume of certain, defined goods. What it lacks is knowledge of the orders that have yet to be placed.

For an indication of this Production has to turn to Marketing. Here then is a valuable point of contact: Marketing says what will be required in future, and Production makes its dispositions accordingly. In practice however what should be an essential step in the production process and one where Marketing can take a lead, is often another source of conflict and misunderstanding. Sometimes this springs from confusion about the nature of the forecast provided and sometimes from a lack of openness about the forecasting process and the uncertainties it entails. There may also be a genuine clash of interest when Marketing cannot predict what the factory would like to see, but that too stems from a misunderstanding which Marketing has to correct.

Long-term forecasts

If we look first at long-term sales forecasts it is clear both that they have to be made, in order that the company as a whole can produce a business plan, and that a large element of uncertainty is involved. If the forecast is contributed by Marketing without explanation and is therefore treated on an 'arm's length' basis by other heads of departments, a fair amount of horse-trading may follow. Chief executives have a habit of bidding-up what they take to be over-cautious estimates of sales, just as they attempt to force down predictions of factory cost. So both Marketing and Production will have reservations about the figures finally agreed. There is no meeting of minds and each department makes its own interpretation of what is really likely to happen.

There is no way in which long-term forecasting can be made an exact science. Five- or ten-year projections are notoriously fallible and even an annual forecast is subject to too many variables to be secure. If successive Chancellors of the Exchequer cannot get it right, how can we expect a marketing manager to do any better? Well, one way could be to accept the uncertainties involved and to explain the basis on which the forecast has been made.[1]

Historical records of sales exist or can be created in sufficient detail to cover all products in the range individually. Records of enquiries and of the conversion ratios of enquiries : orders which apply to each product can also be studied. Trends can be identified and married to predictions of the growth or decline of the market as a whole and of the company's share. The impact of economic factors or of

[1] A more detailed examination of the long-term forecasting process is made in Chapter 3.

government legislation can be taken into account, as can knowledge of competitors' products or promotional plans. In the ultimate there is the forecaster's feel for the future. All of these aspects can be openly discussed with Production. They matter to the factory just as much as they do to the sales force. If there is a range of uncertainty within which the forecast falls, the higher and lower limits of this should also be discussed and their implications explored.

Shorter-term forecasts

Long-term forecasts are likely to be once-a-year or once-a-crisis events. The factory is churning out products every day, and needs more immediate and detailed information to guide it in this than an annual forecast can supply. So shorter term forecasts are often prepared, breaking figures for each product down by model, size, colour and so on. These can be updated as frequently as the length of the production cycle demands. This provides a further opportunity for Production and Marketing to work together. Surprisingly the chance is not always taken, especially in smaller firms.

A key question to ask is how materials are ordered. Usually some stock is kept, and a fresh order issued when a glance at the records, or at the shelves, indicates that a reorder level has been reached. The whole business of reorder levels and determining the quantity to be ordered can be based on factory records of production quantities and of lead times required by suppliers. But it would be most unwise to do this. If the sales department is anticipating an increase or decrease in orders, or a change in customer preferences, or is planning a campaign featuring a particular model, past production experience may prove a poor guide to the future.

Forecasts are not orders

The implication of using forecasts as a guide is that updating has to take place in good time, or sufficient safety margins applied to enable it to work as such. Forecasts are not orders and need to be made far enough in advance to ensure that orders can be met if placed. Marketing and Production can establish frequency of update together, to secure the flexibility necessary to meet changes in demand. The possibility of error can also be discussed. It is certain that detailed forecasts of the type described here will be wrong in some respects, and any critical areas – for example where components are hard to obtain – can be examined in advance.

What will have been gained by this process is yet another route to bringing the customer's requirements closer to the production process. Yet it cuts both ways. If the factory sees a gap in its programme looming sufficiently far ahead it can advise Marketing so that special efforts can be made to find orders for that period.

Product profitability analysis

Another point at which the interests of Marketing and Production overlap is in product costing. From the factory's angle the cost at which various items are produced is an important measure of efficiency. To marketing managers cost is an essential foundation for pricing, and thus forms part of a vital element in the marketing mix. Now there are pricing theorists who would deny that cost is the basis of the price at which things are sold. Surely, it will be said, price is what the market will pay for a given product, regardless of what it costs to make it. But to accept this would imply that in a market with any sensitivity at all to price, the level rapidly falls to that of the cheapest competitor, even if he gets his sums wrong and goes bust in the process of getting a larger share of the business available. In practice studies that have been made of how firms actually fix prices show cost as the starting point,[1] although margins may be, and often are, subsequently modified by market considerations. It can hardly be otherwise, for in real life a marketing manager may be pricing hundreds of items and needs a rule of thumb in most instances. So, in one way or another, a percentage is added to the cost of the finished product.

This percentage is rarely the same for all products. The market insists on modifications, because price sensitivity may be greater for some products than for others, while some competitors may be able to produce certain types of product more cheaply. A company therefore needs to study differences in profitability across the range of all its products. For this accurate information is needed.

Even in the factory it may not be easy to obtain such information. Less popular products attract any stray cost that is around as in the 'dustbin' jobs referred to on page 22 so care has to be taken to see that the figures provided reflect the true situation. But this is not the end of the story because costs of selling and distribution vary

---

Atkin, B. and R.N. Skinner (1975), *How British Industry Prices*, Industrial Market Research Ltd., London.

between products. It might be that a product which is economical to make demands a heavy promotional expense, or absorbs a great deal of time and effort in installation and after-sales service.

An exercise to establish relative profitability across the range can therefore become complex, and require the help of accountants as well as the efforts of marketing and production managers. It is a joint activity which should be followed by joint consideration of the results obtained. Possibly some products should be dropped altogether. Others should perhaps be featured more prominently in the sales programme. There may be some which are at the moment costly and difficult to make, but which sell well. Then a cost reduction exercise could be appropriate. At the end of the day Production and Marketing should be working to a common understanding of where the company's best interests lie.

If all this sounds easy experience shows that it is not. As has been indicated the attribution of cost, and especially of overheads both inside and outside the factory, is open to argument. Unless communication is good, it is quite possible for the factory to be favouring one product and the sales force another. This is where the marketing function, as distinct from sales, has to exercise influence, possibly in both directions.

Product discipline

One of the most useful roles a product manager can play is in maintaining product discipline. This is especially so where a field sales force is employed. Customers are not always ready to take what is offered as it stands, and may request something a little different. If, in their eagerness to obtain orders, sales people simply accept such requests, what was envisaged as a steady run of standard products can become a series of small batches, each differing from the others in some degree.

Some companies are geared to this type of work, and serve their customers best by providing the variety demanded. Others, such as many firms in the construction industry, deal entirely in 'one-offs' where everything is made to measure. But even in extreme cases there is usually a standard element that defines the nature of the company's business, be it in the materials used, the type of designs accommodated or the contract terms deemed acceptable. To move outside these parameters usually entails some loss of profit. For organizations basing their profit predictions on long, unbroken runs of production, the acceptance of too many variations has more serious consequences.

Generally there has to be an element of discipline on the sales side if marketing means more than simply collecting orders regardless of profit. Production units would often like to see this as an absolutely rigid, Henry Ford type of discipline. Marketors, faced with customers who can place their business elsewhere if their requests are rejected, require greater flexibility.

A workable solution in many instances is to divide products into categories such as:

- standard
- non-standard
- special.

Standard is just what the factory, and Henry Ford, would like to make. *Specials* are products which need careful, individual estimates of cost and may involve some development work. A case has to be made for accepting orders for specials, so they would automatically be referred to the product manager or marketing manager who would consult with Production before any promises were made.

By introducing the *non-standard* category a firm may well achieve a reasonable balance between the demands of the market and the needs of the factory. Non-standard products can differ in a number of ways – colour, size, capacity, features – but the range is limited to that for which no additional development is needed and for which costs are known. Such products may be offered on the same terms as standard items, or with differentials in price, discounts, delivery time or size of order accepted.

Marketing has a part to play in maintaining discipline when it comes to selling goods and accepting orders, and in ensuring that the factory is willing to introduce the more flexible routines needed to handle non-standard work.

As a young product manager I was made aware of the size of this task and of the need to use what skills of persuasion I had in accomplishing it. We had an administrative and sales department in London, and a large typewriter factory in Glasgow. Distance, and what might be seen as regional characteristics, made relationships difficult. The factory would have preferred to make all the machines with the same carriage length, the same size of type and even the same typeface. In practice a restricted range was offered which covered most typing requirements. The sales force, however, faced occasional demands for longer carriages to take wide paper, special type sizes, large or small, and special characters for those customers eccentric enough to want to type in foreign languages or use mathematical symbols.

The large and formidable Scot who ran the plant treated all such requests as out-and-out specials, to be entered into the production programme when a gap appeared, and to be built from scratch. So customers might have to wait as long as six months for their machines. On the sales side the complaint was that these machines were often ordered by large customers who also bought dozens of more conventional typewriters. Frustration at long, and often uncertain, delays could lead them to place their routine business elsewhere.

A product profitability analysis indicated that these unusual machines were not unprofitable, even without their less tangible effect on other business. I decided that it would be worth trying to find a better way of handling such orders. It took many journeys in the night sleeper to Glasgow and long days in the factory learning how typewriters were made, but eventually the factory manager and I together found a solution. The common element in all machines was identified and a small working stock of 'carcasses' built to this level was created. A sales forecast of extra long carriages was made and an inventory of these was assembled. Individual characters were more of a problem but this too had a solution at reasonable cost. After that it was possible to inject orders into a standard production run whenever required. What had been specials were reclassified as non-standard, and delivery was reduced from six months to three weeks.

This was of course no great engineering feat. It could have been done at any time by the people at the plant. But they would not have done it of their own accord, because they did not see the need. Nor would they have done it simply at the request of a newly fledged product manager. Sitting at a desk in London demanding shorter delivery times would have produced either no response at all, or good technical reasons why it was not possible.

In my inexperience I had stumbled on the one way to make things happen, which was to carry marketing into the factory and work with the managers there to identify and solve a common problem. The difficult part was over once the problem was recognized as such by everyone concerned.

Delivery discipline

In transactions of this kind an implicit bargain is struck between Production and Marketing. This is that Production will deliver in the time stated and that Marketing will not promise delivery in a shorter time. It is often not an easy bargain to keep.

On the sales side pressure may come from customers whose needs are genuinely urgent. It may also be inspired by competitors offering quicker delivery. If competitors are themselves undisciplined, the promises they make can be quite unrealistic, however attractive they appear to the customer. Selling against this type of opposition creates temptations, especially for commission-hungry sales representatives. Do they stick to what they believe to be true, and lose the order? Or do they take an optimistic view of delivery dates, knowing that they will not be able to complete the order on time, but certain that their competitors' promises are even farther fetched?

One of the benefits of interposing a marketing or product manager between the sales force and the factory is that it makes it easier to resist pressures of this kind. For resisted they must be, if every order is not to become a priority, as customers clamour to receive deliveries which are overdue once the date given has been passed. The factory then begins to chase its tail and the production manager falls into a cynical frame of mind, which tends to hamper efforts to meet the really urgent cases that do, of course, arise.

At one time failure to meet delivery promises was endemic in British industry. The struggle to emerge from that unhappy state has been long and hard. To maintain an attitude towards performance which implies that delivery next Wednesday means exactly that, and not Thursday or Friday, still requires continuous effort. The part that Marketing has to play is clear, if difficult at times. It is even more difficult for Production. There the problem lies in ensuring not only that all workers accept the obligation to perform on time, but that all suppliers do so as well.

In the past a production manager might have felt that the failure of others to produce materials or parts on time in same way exonerated the factory from its obligations. This was in fact the mechanism by which the virus of non-performance was transmitted throughout industry. Once excuses are not accepted at any level the disease is checked. Alternative suppliers who keep to time have to be found whenever a significant failure occurs. If the managers of both production and marketing departments are at one on this issue alone, many of the personal and organizational problems that might otherwise bedevil relationships will tend to fade away.

Naturally there are risks in expounding what might appear to be an absolutist view of performance in a world where banana skins abound. But on this issue I would recommend for any doubters a short course of work experience as a subcontractor to the construction industry. Here the customer, usually a main contractor, is large and the supplier small. The contract contains penalties for non-performance which may exceed the value of the order. Where a large order is involved, failure to give a correct date and to keep to it can mean not the loss of future business, but the closure of the business itself. Similar situations exist where any smaller company supplies a limited number of larger, more powerful customers. So we are not considering something which is out of practical reach, but something which is happening every day in companies where management effort is fully integrated.

Quality procedures

Recent years have seen an improvement in quality procedures that has matched, and often contributed to, improved performance in other aspects of manufacturing. Technology has played a major part in securing greater reliability, as well as in providing more advanced testing equipment. But a good deal has been done to spread awareness of the need for quality more widely among the work-force.

It would be a mistake to think of this movement as marketing led. Many developments have stemmed from advances in engineering as, for example, the use of robots which change the role of the machine operator to something more like that of an inspector. The appearance in the market-place of more reliable products has stimulated demand and created expectations that may not have been apparent before. Rather than customers making their presence felt in the factory, the factory has reached out to the customer and offered something better. This is turn has become a measure by which other products are judged.

Where Marketing can play a part is in assessing the weight placed on quality at any given time, and in advising which aspects of quality (finish, long life, reliability, short downtime, etc.) have the greatest appeal to customers. For improvements to a product are seldom without cost, and customers might well be prepared to trade some aspects of quality for a lower price. Markets can often be segmented into top, medium and basic quality sectors. When this is so Marketing can weigh the benefits of positioning a product in any given sector, so that the product and its cost can be tailored accordingly. As has been suggested previously, it can also conduct research to check how customers rate the product against those of competitors. In this way Marketing acts as the eyes and ears of the factory.

We should also consider the wider approach to quality embodied in standards such as BS 5750. This is primarily a paperwork system. The completion of various records at all stages of the production process is both its main method of operation and the evidence that a given company complies with the standard. Clearly it is possible to have reservations about the efficacy of paperwork in redirecting attitudes or determining actual standards of workmanship. But a positive aspect of BS 5750 is that it directs attention to the need to ensure that the customer gets exactly what was ordered, and not an approximation. This is one area where, especially in firms supplying custom-built products, divergences can appear between ideas of what is required held by Marketing, the drawing office and the shop floor. A system which puts the onus on Marketing to establish precisely what its customer wants, and on Production to provide just that, is simply organized common sense.

Customer visits

One of the most direct ways of bringing customers closer to the factory is to invite them to visit it. This can be done anywhere but is of course particularly appropriate where the product is, to any significant degree, built to order. A boat builder, for example, can show a customer not just boats in general, but his, her or their own boat in the course of construction. What is gained by this? For the boat builder it can be the establishment of confidence in the product and its makers, such as will sustain relationships when the inevitable snags and queries arise. In the boat-building industry loyal customers are important to future business and their boats are floating showrooms. Yet chocolate makers also welcome visits to help create the image of a wholesome and tasty product and to reinforce brand loyalty.

There is also benefit to be gained from listening to what customers or potential customers have to say. Production people seldom get face-to-face communication of this kind. Most companies would prefer to have someone from Marketing present on these occasions, both to handle sales questions if they arise and to help interpret comments made, since Marketing should be able to judge just how representative a particular customer's views may be.

Installation

In a number of cases the production process is not really complete until the product is installed and working. Examples extend from the construction industry to machine tools or computer systems. Often special installation staff are employed. These are the people the customer sees. At a critical time the image of the company, which has up to then been sustained by marketing personnel, falls into the hands of someone else. The question is, what should Marketing do about that?

Control of field activity

In one sense there is little for Marketing to do. If the installation job is carried out efficiently, the customer has obtained what was wanted and, as far as that order goes, Marketing's original objective has been achieved. Furthermore in most companies the importance of installation work is fully appreciated if only because payment hangs upon it. As a result control of activity in the field receives a good deal of attention.

The advent of mobile communications has made day-to-day supervision easier, and there are in addition several ways to measure performance, such as the time taken the complete the job and the cost of any remedial work which may follow. Feedback from customers is likely to be swift and vocal at this stage if any problems occur on site. As an additional precaution it is sometimes useful to get employees from the factory to handle a number of installations, partly to give them a feel for the completed product, but also to obtain a yardstick by which the performance of specialist installation teams can be judged.

The hired cowboy

Control of activity becomes more important where self-employed installers are used. Installation is an area where free enterprise has flourished. Many companies find it uneconomic to maintain their own installation teams. Gaps between orders, a potential clash of delivery dates, or geographical problems can all cause difficulties. So specialist installers have multiplied, either serving local districts or offering a degree of mobility hard to find among a firm's own employees. Some of these have been little more than hired 'cowboys', and the damage this type of installer can do to the reputation of a manufacturer is considerable. So although in the majority of cases the system may work well, inspection of the finished work is necessary to ensure that standards are being maintained.

The role of Marketing

So what is it that Marketing can add to a situation that should already be well under control? Clearly the one thing that is not needed is marketing people on site impeding the efforts of installers with a job to do. The very presence of sales staff at this stage can invite last minute changes of mind on the part of the customer that generally result in no one's satisfaction. The role is more advisory. Installers, including any hired from outside, need to be trained to look and act like an integral part of the company that they are representing at a crucial moment in its relationship with its customers. Overalls, where appropriate, can enhance this image. Vehicles and tool kits can carry the firm's logo and be kept so that they look proud of it. Small but significant points of behaviour, for example cleaning up after a job, can be emphasized in training and checked by periodic inspections. Above all installers can be instructed in how to answer the sort of questions that may be asked, and which questions to refer back to the marketing department. And in the longer term Marketing can, through simple surveys, assess the company's reputation as an installer and report its findings, so that any necessary improvements can be made.

Service

In several ways the relationship between Marketing and after-sales service is similar to that between Marketing and Installation. The strongest ways in which marketing influence can be brought to bear are likely to be indirect. Chiefly this means persuading the company as a whole of the significance of after-sales service in obtaining future business, and in providing advice and training on behaviour in front of the customer. There are however two important differences when considering service as opposed to installation. One is contained in the very nature of the service job; the other results from a perceived opportunity to use service personnel more directly in a selling role.

The person who services equipment in the field sees all its faults, and sometimes in the process forgets its virtues. So even if he or she refrains from saying: 'Oh yes, Sir, that's a common fault with these models. We've had no end of trouble with them,' eyes, expression and tone of voice may say almost as much. A certain cynicism, often combined with a desire to display technical knowledge of the product, can have a depressing effect on customers. Paradoxically, service people with real diagnostic skills seldom behave like this. Their job satisfaction lies in being able to fix all and any problems that arise. But diagnostic ability of this level is rare, and when a cynical attitude is allied to a less-than-perfect technical grasp, the result is a marketor's nightmare.

Service people have therefore to be trained as representatives of the company. Their objectives have to be consistent with the company's marketing aims. As far as customers are concerned the objective for service personnel then becomes to remove all potential worries and doubts, and in one call, if at all possible. Better technical training and the confidence this brings will do most to achieve this. Where Marketing can help is often in some straightforward training in handling the human side of a service call.

Service or sales force?

Once this is achieved there is a temptation to go further. Service people are face to face with customers for a substantial part of each working day. Customers are also potential customers for other products in the range or for new and updated versions of the product in use. Can we not then make people who are already representatives of the company into something more like sales representatives? Could they not be seen as a sales force, already deployed in the field, with ready access to a receptive market?

There are several ways of developing this theme. Service people could be given a franchise to sell certain products, or could be paid an introductory commission on any business they originate, or could be encouraged in other ways to bring in sales enquiries.

It has been my fate in the past to be subjected to all manner of plausible suggestions for increasing business painlessly by one or other of these routes. In reality there are few painless ways of obtaining business. Most schemes for combining sales and service functions underrate the boost to sales that an effective service organization brings in its own right. This can be imperilled by anything which undermines the trust between a customer and the person who looks after the equipment that has been purchased.

A high degree of selling skill is needed to switch roles in the middle of a service call. Anyone with this skill might well consider a selling job as an alternative to service work. For the majority the best results have seemed to come from the use of eyes and ears to spot sales opportunities, which are then passed quietly on to colleagues in Marketing.

Any scheme more elaborate or formal than this may not only impair relations with customers, but also set up rivalry between the service staff and the sales force. It is important that clear objectives for service, leading to an identifiable form of job satisfaction should not be subverted by schemes offering an often illusory chance of 'a fast buck'.

The problem of new products

A further point at which Marketing and Service need to observe caution and work closely together is when a new product is introduced. The sales force may see it as an opportunity, but unless positive steps are taken the service department could see it as a threat. Here after all is something new, for which no corpus of diagnostic experience has been built up, yet for which Service has responsibility from day one. What is worse, initial sales may be slow or scattered, so that in any given service area there may be wide gaps between calls and little opportunity to put into effect whatever training has been given.

It is therefore not enough for a marketing manager in charge of a product launch to ensure that service training is given in good time. Close liaison with the service department is needed for an extended period, to see that early service experience is analysed and that refresher training is provided wherever necessary. Some persuasion will be needed to ensure this, since it will cost money quite disproportionate to the amount of equipment yet in use. If it is not done, however, the new product's reputation can suffer unnecessary damage at a critical stage. This kind of situation tests the faith that a marketing manager has in the future of the product he or she has launched.

Movement of personnel

In discussing the need for marketing people to work closely with colleagues in Production, Installation or Service certain obstacles have been identified. These may be geographical, cultural or functional. Together they can constitute a formidable barrier. In time it may become an article of faith that someone who works in Sales is somehow different from someone in Production, who is in turn different from someone in the service department: so different on occasion that people outside any given department are seen not as individual humans at all, but as stereotypes.

Invisible barriers

Reference has been made to the way in which both marketing and production departments may feel that they, and only they, are at the sharp end of the business. It is a comparatively short step from this to a point of view which sees other departments merely as obstacles in a process that would otherwise run smoothly, and drains their members of humanity. Thereafter they become at best objects for manipulation, not people working to a common purpose.

Marketing has to take the initiative in crossing this invisible barrier, and some entry points have been identified. If however the barrier itself can be weakened the task will be easier. One approach to this is through movement of personnel around the company. No one is born a production worker or a sales clerk, although a variety of educational and cultural influences, as well as pure chance, may have pointed in that direction. He or she might succeed just as well or better in another role, given an interest in doing so and the opportunity to try it.

Cross-links at various levels

If installation staff have had firsthand experience of manufacturing, or if a sales representative has worked in the service department or in the factory, cross-links are formed below managerial level which make for smoother relationships. Perhaps more importantly, since instances of this kind will be comparatively few, the idea that there is no impediment to movement between departments is given credence. This is not only encouraging for career-minded individuals, but helps to promote the concept of the company as a collection of people working in what are, for the time being, different ways, but towards a common goal. Actual movement achieves more in this direction than any number of well-turned phrases by chairman or chief executive.

Promoting the idea

Some care needs to be taken in promoting movement between departments. There is no point at all in losing a good installer in order to gain an ineffective sales representative. Furthermore although no one's present job was ordained from on high, the disruption of leaving it may be more than some otherwise well-qualified people can accept.

Once, at a time of rapid expansion in the electronics industry, I scoured the company to find suitable candidates for jobs in the marketing department. I was looking for potential product managers. One of the key qualifications for this job was, I thought, the ability to think clearly about issues which were often surrounded and obscured by emotion. Evidence of this ability was sometimes obtainable from a person's academic record, but not every one of our 1500 employees had an academic record.

We had however already had a good deal of success in identifying clear thinkers who had escaped the educational net, by the use of various intelligence tests. The one which seemed at the time most appropriate for the positions I had in mind was the Watson–Glaser Critical Thinking Appraisal. Its use had previously revealed a number of suitable candidates whose abilities, without it, might have been overlooked.

Of course critical thinking was not all that was needed. Imagination, persuasive skills and determination to see a job through were also required. In my opinion no reliable tests for these qualities had yet been published, so I embarked on an extensive interview programme, in the course of which the Watson–Glaser test was administered.

The quality of the people tested was generally high, but one candidate ran right off the top of the scale in the Watson–Glaser appraisal. He was a service engineer living in Wales and had almost the ideal profile for the job I had in mind. The only snag was that he was wedded to his locality, where he ran the Boys' Brigade, and had no desire at all to move, or to practise skills he had not realized he possessed.

In facilitating movement within the firm it is as well to appreciate that the best may indeed lack all ambition, if not conviction, and that the worst can quite easily display a passionate intensity, or perhaps plain greed.

What is needed is not a programme to shuffle people round the company on a routine basis, or to promote from within to the exclusion of suitable candidates from outside. It is rather an enabling procedure, to ensure that job opportunities are known to all, and that movement within the company is regarded as a natural part of life. Once this is accepted without fuss by all departments, some erosion of the blue–white divide has already been achieved.

Questions and action points for decision takers

Sources of conflict

Where are the production, installation and service departments situated relative to Marketing:

- in the same building
- on different floors
- in a different part of the site
- miles away from each other?

How often do the managers of each department visit their counterparts:

- daily
- weekly
- monthly
- hardly ever?

Have these visits produced an in-depth understanding?

What knowledge of the company's marketing policies do production workers/supervisors have?

How can this be checked?

What conflicts between Marketing and Production do you know of?

Could there be others?

Is there a role for a product manager?

Product management

If not, who is responsible for the functions of product management?

What market research has been done, or is planned, to check the status of the product in the market place?

Have the results been communicated to:

- production management
- the work force as a whole?

Better use of sales forecasts

What long term forecasts of sales have been made?

Have they, and the basis on which they were compiled, been discussed with production management?

What shorter term forecasts are provided by Marketing for Production?

How often are they updated?

Is this period correct, in the light of the time needed to change production levels?

Is the distinction between forecasts and orders fully appreciated?

Product profitability

Is there an analysis of the profitability of different products in the range?

Does this include selling and distribution costs as well as the cost of production?

What policies exist towards the sale/production of products carrying different margins?

Are decisions on these matters taken jointly by Marketing and Production?

Product disciplines

Who tells the sales department what may or may not be sold?

Have products been categorized as standard, non-standard and special or in some equivalent way?

Who controls the delivery times quoted?

Are these agreed and accepted by both marketing and production managers?

How does Production ensure that delivery times are maintained?

What quality procedures are in force?

Are they related to engineering standards or to the needs of customers (as revealed through market research)?

What procedures are in place to ensure that the customer receives exactly what has been ordered?

Are there opportunities for customers to visit the factory?

How is installation work controlled?

What has been done to present installers as an integral part of the company?

Has advice been obtained from Marketing on this?

What training has been given to service staff in customer relations?

Are there any schemes afoot to involve service people in selling?

If so, have the consequences been fully explored?

In the case of new products, what plans are made for marketing/service liaison?

Over what period do these extend?

Movement between departments

Have any marketing people had experience in other departments, or vice versa?

Is movement between departments accepted as normal throughout the company?

If not, how could it be promoted?

3

Joining the dots
How to get accountants involved in marketing

Engineers, production managers and marketors have their differences, but they stand united on one point, a general dislike of accountants. It is general and not particular because they will know individual accountants against whom they harbour no hard feelings, and may even share a drink or a meal with them from time to time. But for accountants as a breed feelings range from weary acceptance to genuine loathing. Outside the profession it is considered a serious insult to accuse a fellow executive of 'thinking like an accountant'.

What have accountants done to earn this reputation? They are accused of 'considering only the bottom line', 'thinking only of money, not people', 'knowing nothing about the (real) business', 'lacking imagination' and 'thinking short term only'. In turn they would probably answer that they are only doing their job, which is to apply professional standards and disciplines to a business that would otherwise run off the rails, especially if left to the direction of emotive and innumerate leaders. So the lines of conflict are drawn in advance of any actual issues that may arise.

A Treasury model?

To some extent this is a matter of money and of rival claims to the allocation of resources. A similar situation exists in government, when budgets are being prepared. Spending departments demand more money for what each sees as vital projects, while the Treasury strives to keep expenditure under control. In a company the accountant in charge of the financial budget will see Production, Development, Sales or Advertising as cost centres. If cost can be restrained in the face of their vociferous demands for more resources, then by simple arithmetic the company will make more profit. On rare occasions really dedicated accountants will even see themselves as cost centres, but that cost is invariably justified by the need to keep an eye on the expenses of others.

The heart of the business

There is however more to the animosity generated between accountants and others than just money. What is at stake is where the heart of the business is thought to lie. In its crudest terms Engineering may see this in the creation of a worthy product, while the marketor may see it in the conquest of new markets. Such approaches tend to be emotive. Indeed they must be if they are to be successful, for they are unlikely to work without a belief that the activity involved, whether in creating products or in conquering markets, really *matters*, to the company for certain, and very likely to the community at large.

Against them stands the accountant. Essentially a realist, the accountant is looking at profit and loss statements, debtors and creditors and, yes, the bottom line. For here must lie whatever heart the company has. Products and people alike are tools for fashioning profit. This in the ultimate means the satisfaction of the shareholders, to whom the business belongs, or the bankers to whom it is pledged.

Within the company it is not going to be easy to reconcile these differing views. I have met very few departmental managers in businesses of any size who gave a hoot for the interests of shareholders or bankers. Yet there are two general considerations which help to take the heat from the argument, and to prepare the way for a more detailed discussion of the steps that lead to reconciliation.

First it has to be said that the heart of any company is unlikely to remain in a fixed position. In other words the style of leadership and the department best placed to give a lead, should change over time, in order to be appropriate to the situation in which the company actually stands. Companies pass through stages of growth, maturity and decline. In a pioneering phase the impetus probably comes from innovative engineering or aggressive marketing. In a period of consolidation efficient production and programmes to reduce product cost may be the key to success. On the downslope the concentration should be on trimming unprofitable lines and maximizing profit in more favourable areas. The best person to pioneer growth is hardly likely to be ideal at squeezing the last drops of profit in a period of decline. So decisions about leadership, or about the relative influence different departments should exercise, need to be related to specific stages in a company's development if these can be identified.

Secondly it can be argued that whoever is currently, and correctly, in charge, whether it be marketor, engineer or accountant, at all stages it is accountants who provide a means of measuring success. Profit may be a crude yardstick for human endeavour, but it is a more comprehensive test than factory output or market share. It enables comparisons to be made both within and beyond any given industry. In consequence even those whose loyalty leans more to their employees than to their shareholders accept financial criteria as marks on the winning-post.

But however rational it may be to grant accountants their place at all times – and even a leading role at certain critical stages – fear of undue influence persists, and an underlying antipathy remains.

A marketing bugbear

In the case of Marketing, feelings of this sort are rarely far below the surface. They are sharpened by a view of marketing frequently held by accountants. It is partly a matter of professionalism, or of one rather narrow aspect of it. An accountant either is, or wants to be, qualified. Most marketors are not, or have qualifications removed from the role they are now playing. To an accountant, they can appear to hold opinions based on little more than whim, to be essentially profligate in their struggle to succeed, and ephemeral in their tenure of the job. Furthermore it would not be too hard to find examples to justify such a view.

Of course the marketor will see things very differently. To marketing eyes what accountants do is, at best, to count the money others make. At worst they put obstacles in the way of those trying to make it. The day-by-day situation is often frustrating, because the advantage in any specific argument over money always lies with the accountant. Accounts covering marketing or sales activity can be scrutinized at leisure and any item of expense queried at length. Marketing, in contrast, neither has nor would normally wish to have the ability or the time to investigate in detail the operations of the accounts department.

It is against this background that we shall be looking for ways of integrating the efforts of these two limbs of the company. Initially it is easier to see points of conflict than opportunities to work together. From strategic issues such as the company's business plan, through advertising expenditure, to the use made of sales representatives' cars, there is ample scope for disagreement. Yet there are benefits to be gained by Marketing, and by the company as a whole, from demolishing this particular barrier. And the initiative will have to come from Marketing if these benefits are to be secured.

Strategic issues

The first point at which a meeting of minds can be sought is in the construction of a business plan. Whether this is for several years ahead or for the next few months it will require a forecast of business to be obtained in the future, and of the marketing costs involved in obtaining it. It is important for marketors to appreciate how accountants are likely to treat these matters, and to be ready to explain and justify their own approach.

Joining the dots

Accountants will base their opinion of any projected figures firmly in experience of the past. Their work is primarily historical, recording the sales volume achieved and the promotional expense incurred over the same period. The trend of figures for recent months or years serves as a basis for extrapolation into the future. In other words, a line is traced through the dots marking previous sales volume and this line is extended upwards or downwards according to the direction in which it points. Of course for the mathematically inclined there are more sophisticated ways of joining the dots, for example by the use of regression analysis, and allowance may be made for uncertainty on either side of the line. But the starting point is always history.

Similarly with sales expense it is a knowledge of past figures and their ratio to turnover that guide an accountant's thinking. If in the last year or two advertising has amounted to 1 per cent of turnover, that may be taken as a good indication of what should be allowed in the business plan.

Naturally a marketing approach is, or should be, different. It is not a matter of ignoring the historical figures to which both Marketing and Accounts have access: in the absence of any well-found reason why it should be otherwise, the past will have to be taken as a guide. Nor is it a matter of waving a damp finger in the air, or of averaging the guesses of marketors, salesmen or dealers. What Marketing has to have is a sound method for predicting future events, which it must be prepared to demonstrate to colleagues in other departments.

Looking to the future

In forecasting sales this means taking into consideration a number of factors which are not shown in the company's accounts. To approach the task systematically we need to know what potential the market holds for all participants, how far this has already been satisfied, what inroads are likely to be made on the remaining potential in the form of the total annual sales of all competitors combined, and what share of the total we can expect to achieve. To form opinions on each aspect of this calculation, we have to study anything which might influence the market as a whole, or our share of it. Some influencing factors, such as anticipated economic trends or proposed government regulations, may be matters of public knowledge or at least of public speculation. Others, as for example, competitors' determination and ability to defend their market share, call for judgement.

Building a forecast from bricks of this kind is a very different process from joining the dots of past performance. If it is not well understood it can appear to be less precise, if only because it is undeniably more imaginative. It does, however, avoid the serious pitfalls of extrapolation which lie in assuming that the future is merely a continuation of the past. Marketing's task is to make as good a forecast as possible, and then to demonstrate to colleagues the soundness of the reasoning behind the conclusions that have been reached. Because this is not always easy, we will be advised to take a closer look at the bricks that are used and at the way they should be laid.

Potential The term potential is often employed loosely. It can refer to potential annual sales, or to the total potential still to be exploited. But for reasons which will become clear, I shall give it a wider definition than either of these. Potential is the quantity of a given product that would be in the hands of customers if everyone who could use it bought as much as could be used. Once this broad concept is accepted it can be subdivided into:

- *ultimate* potential
- *immediate* potential.

The ultimate potential is as just defined; the immediate potential is that portion of it seen to be accessible to marketing effort in the near future. So the ultimate potential contains the immediate and they may indeed be identical. But if any gap exists between them it should be of great interest to forecasters.

As an example we might take lawnmowers. The ultimate potential for motor driven lawnmowers was always the number of households with lawns. But initially immediate potential was seen as only those households with lawns large enough to justify the expense of a motor mower. A forecast based on all lawns of any size would have been wildly optimistic. In time however the immediate potential grew to the point where virtually all lawn owners were prospects for motor mowers. From this it is clear that judgements about potential are valid only at the time they are made, and must be revised as the market develops.

The relationship between ultimate and immediate potential and other terms we might use in forecasting are shown in Figure 3.1. Here ultimate potential is indicated by the area within circle A and immediate potential is represented by circle B.

Penetration and annual sales Usually some potential will already have been satisfied. This is shown in Figure 3.1 as *penetration* (circle C). Current *annual sales* are indicated by circle D and are those of all competitors, taken together. Within this circle is another, E, which shows new sales as part of the annual total. This is of significance because it distinguishes additional sales, which extend overall penetration and eat into potential, from replacement sales which do not.

Now we have a few bricks in position and can see how they might influence forecasting. So far we have been dealing with the market as a whole, not with our share. If we can predict the way in which the whole market is going to move, it will be much easier to forecast our part of it.

Probably the easiest figure to obtain with reasonable accuracy is that for the total annual sales (Figure 3.1, circle D). If thinking stops at this point we are likely to be engaged in another dot-joining

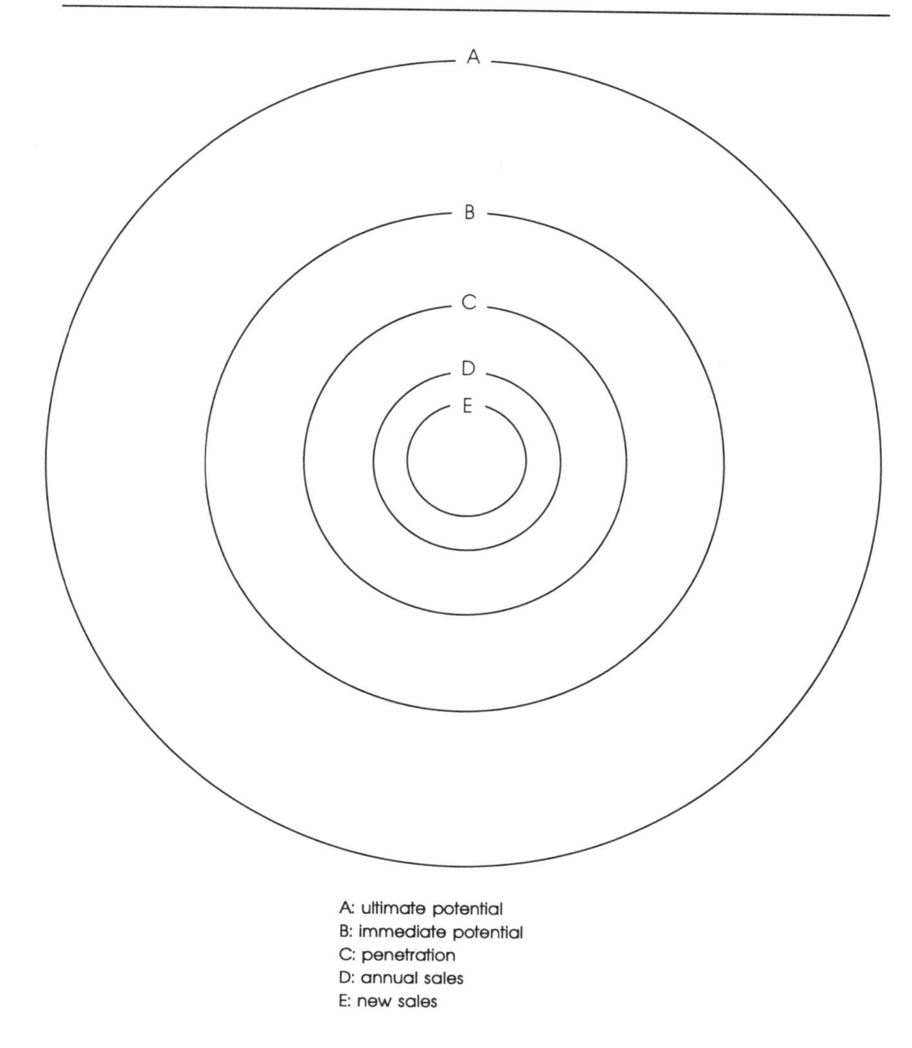

Figure 3.1 Quantitative market analysis

exercise, this time for the market as a whole rather than for our own sales. That would represent an advance, but by itself it could prove inadequate, even dangerous.

Imagine a market where the ultimate potential appears very large and where total annual sales are advancing at, say, 30 per cent per annum. Such a scenario could lead to bullish optimism and encourage companies not yet engaged to participate. Yet the immediate potential could be near to saturation. If this is not realized and all players gear up to a further 30 per cent annual increase, some heads are going to bump against the ceiling. Exactly this happened some years ago in the market for large beverage vending machines. My own company was thinking of entering at the time, and it was a calculation of immediate potential combined with the known trend of annual sales that kept us out. Others were not so fortunate.

Sometimes it happens the other way. Products which have seemed to be struggling against a limited immediate potential have suddenly found their horizons expanded, possibly through technical development. Facsimile machines illustrate both aspects, since original forecasts, based on high estimates of ultimate potential, were far too optimistic, yet there came a time when more reliable, cheaper machines and better transmission lines combined to produce the long promised and long denied leap forward.

Naturally judgement has to be applied to make a sensible estimate of immediate as opposed to ultimate potential. Even a figure for penetration may need some calculation in the absence of reliable published figures. Often it is possible to add annual sales and subtract a proportion for replacement sales, to make an approximation. Great precision is not required. What is needed is an awareness of any aspect of the market that may affect its future progress.

Competitors' shares It is always possible to get some idea of the shares of the total market obtained by competitors. Again great accuracy is not needed to construct a working model. Some markets are widely fragmented, while others may be dominated by two or three major competitors. For a marketor who entertains thoughts of increasing market share, and even more so for one who is contemplating entry into a new market, it is important to know these things. For while it may be easy to establish or increase a share of a fragmented market, a move which threatens serious inroads into the shares already enjoyed by a few key players, is bound to provoke a strong reaction. In a rapidly expanding market this may perhaps be avoided, but in a stable or declining market, pressure on prices seems the most likely outcome.

Some caution is therefore required when establishing the percentage share of the market a sales forecast represents. If you are looking for an increase, spare a thought for your competitors, busy calculating their own forecasts, and each looking for an increase too. Whenever it has been possible to add up the percentage shares to which all participants in an industry are laying claim, the total has always come to more than 100 per cent.

Threats and opportunities So far we have been looking at factors which are to some extent quantifiable. Potential, penetration, annual sales and competitors' shares all interact to influence a forecaster's judgement. Outside these there are other factors which may affect the market as a whole, or sections of it. Sometimes these are favourable. For example, official fire regulations stimulated sales of alarm and detection equipment to shops, offices and hotels to an extent no salesmanship could have been expected to achieve of itself. Sometimes there are threats rather than opportunities, or even cases where an opportunity for one business is a threat to another. Provision for the disabled in public buildings might seem a worthy addition to building regulations. Clearly it is bound to put up construction costs, which will, in many cases increase the profit of builders. But the manufacturers of spiral fire escapes see it as a threat to their product, and as an inhibiting factor in a number of construction projects where space is limited.

The most serious threats to established industries come from the development of alternative ways of satisfying customers' needs. The great age of canals was overtaken by the development of railways almost as soon as the most ambitious and costly canal systems were completed. Now the railways themselves are under siege. The electronics industry has provided opportunities for new companies, armed with chips and software, to enter fields from which they would have been excluded in the electro-mechanical era. It is often hard for companies already established to anticipate the precise direction and timing of threats of this kind. Certainly it is yet another instance of the fallibility of dot-joining as a technique of forecasting. Marketing's job is to be aware of the possibility and alert to the first signs that an existing product is under serious attack.

Adding resources The marketor is not a passive spectator of market movements, threats and opportunities. It is unlikely that past levels of sales have been achieved without promotional effort. Therefore it may be assumed that if more effort is made, more sales will follow. The difficulty lies in deciding how much additional expense is needed and what, if anything, it is likely to produce.

The best way to find out is to experiment by adding resources in trial areas only. For large companies in the consumer field, this is complex, but perfectly feasible. For smaller firms selling to specialized markets, it may not be at all easy. Nevertheless, it is often possible to increase sales coverage, or advertise in new media, and in assessing the results, make allowance for the stray variables that inevitably attend such exercises.

What is certain is that a forecast of substantially increased sales, based solely on the assumed effect of higher promotional expense without any evidence that it will actually work, will be received with scepticism.

Putting it together

In summary the marketing department, if it is doing its job, will in the case of every product be considering:

- potential, both ultimate and immediate
- penetration to date
- the trend of annual sales
- the split between new and replacement business
- the shares of competitors
- overall economic trends
- legislative requirements or regulations
- alternative technology and convergence
- the effect of additional promotion.

as well as the past sales record of the company, statistics of enquiries received and so on. The list is not exhaustive, and according to circumstances some factors may need much more care and attention than others. Marketing has to look at anything that might affect sales before compiling a forecast. Some of the answers obtained will be estimates, based on whatever facts are available and on the use of appropriate analogies where necessary. The final result will have a degree of probability that will vary with the state of turbulence of the market.

Two sorts of professional?

Now is the time for the marketing manager to explain to his or her colleagues and especially to the accountant, how the forecast was compiled and what level of confidence can be placed in it. If the nature of the thinking process can be made clear, the results may come to be accepted, and the accountant can then carry the budget right down to the bottom line. If there are reasonable doubts and perhaps upper and lower limits of confidence, alternative budgets can be prepared, so that all consequences can be thoroughly explored. Accountants and marketors are then working together, and it is tempting to imagine that each side will recognize professionalism in the other.

For two reasons it is doubtful if, even at best, it will be quite like this. In the first place accountants, or honest ones at any rate, tend to have reservations about creative figure-work, and that is what Marketing has produced. Secondly, the very nature of the forecasting process outlined above points in a different direction. If marketing were a profession it might be assumed that two different marketing managers, presented with the same facts, or lack of facts, would produce similar forecasts. In practice they would almost certainly not do so. Marketing is more like a craft than a traditional profession, and the respect it earns should be that accorded to the skilled craftsman.

Long or short term

Once mutual respect is established it will be much easier to work with Accounts on budgets or wider business plans. There may however still be questions to resolve about whether the company should be looking for long- or short-term benefits.

It is possible that Marketing may envisage good growth in years to come, based on considerable expense in the near future. Almost any new product will bring about such a situation, as will, in all likelihood, expansion into new markets, or a determined assault on a larger market share. The uncertainty and risk involved will be weighed by others against a more cautious strategy which could show greater profit in the next year or two. This is a common field of battle between marketors and accountants. It might help for Marketing to appreciate that there is nothing inherently wrong in thinking short term. A company has every right to take profit now and not later, and may have pressures upon it to do so. A case has therefore to be made for a longer-term approach and for the extra risks attached to it. It is wise in making such a case to point out the risks of attempting to stand still as well as those of the proposed course of action. If the right relationships have been established there is no reason why positive discussions should not be held with accountants, who can help a great deal in preparing a detailed proposal for the chief executive.

Warming cold feet

Relationships will be tested when predictions made are not fulfilled. Naturally no sales forecast is ever correct in every detail, but there are times when things appear to be going seriously awry. Take the case of a new product. It is notoriously difficult to forecast demand in the early stages of a product, and false starts are quite common. The selling cycle may prove to be longer than anticipated, so that initial sales appear disappointing, although there could be rapid improvement when quotations mature. At the other extreme advanced publicity or a delay to the launch can create a pent-up demand, which leads to a rush of sales in the early days that might not be sustained. These two situations are illustrated in Figure 3.2 (a), (b). The long-term trend is the same in both cases, but in (a) sales move slowly at first, so that by the time point P is reached accountants, production managers and chief executives alike are prone to take a pessimistic view. In (b) the reverse applies and undue optimism may prevail for a time, to be followed by a collapse in confidence until sales right themselves.

If at such times the management team, or any influential member of it, shows signs of anxiety, enthusiasm throughout the firm may suffer. And once this extends to the sales force the pessimists may well find their worst prophecies fulfilled. A marketor will need more than ice-cold nerves to steady his or her colleagues at such times. Accountants in particular are likely to prove sceptical when faced with the concrete facts in front of them.

The information that will help to diagnose what is happening, and what may be expected in the near future could include:

- Customers so far obtained: are larger orders to follow?
- Outstanding quotations: how much business do they realistically represent?
- Prospective customers: are we yet in contact with the most lucrative sectors of the market?
- Enquiries: at what rate are they currently being received?
- Advertising: is there more to come? what is the response time following an insertion?
- Length of selling cycle: first contact to order.
- Sales activity: how much effort is being directed to this particular product?
- Sales performance: of branches, teams, individuals.

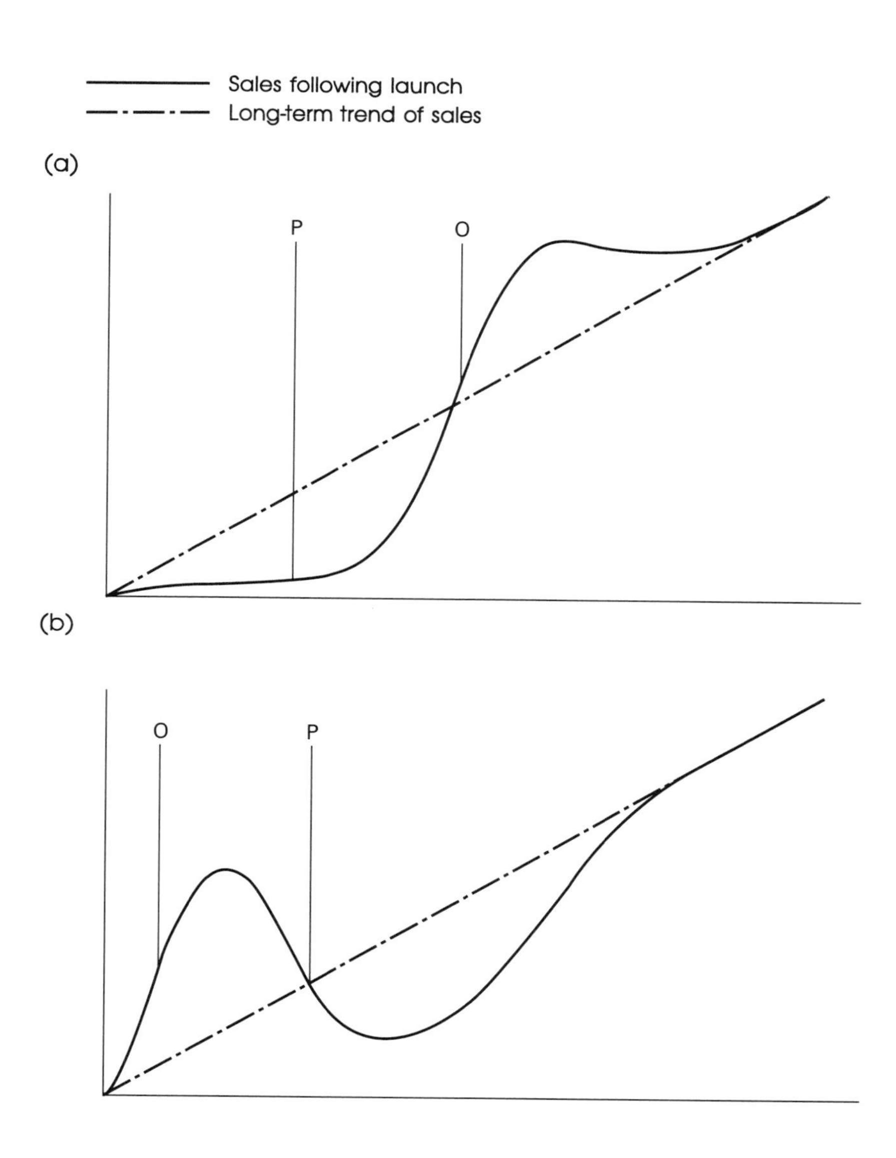

O = Point at which figures encourage undue optimism
P = Point at which figures encourage undue pessimism

Figure 3.2 False starts following a new product launch

An examination of some or all of these factors could help to confirm the longer-term trend of business, as well as to indicate any action necessary to deal with the current situation.

What is in fact happening here is that Marketing is again practising the skills of its craft. This time the information to be studied is more immediate. It should have been collected from the day the product was launched. But again there are no certainties in the conclusions reached, only judgements. The onus is on Marketing to explain the basis of such judgements. At times of crisis this is likely to be more effective than a stiff upper lip, and much more persuasive than vague promises that all will eventually go well. By adopting an open approach Marketing is in essence teaching other departments to speak its language, just as it has to learn to speak the language of engineering or accountancy.

Tactical issues

It is sometimes the case that while accountants and marketors may be able to see eye to eye on strategic policy, below this level some sniping still occurs. There are after all several good targets for accountants to shoot at.

Advertising is one, both because its results are occasionally hard to quantify and because expenditure on it is inherently 'lumpy'. Some months show little or no advertising expense, then when a campaign is held and the bills come in, several major payments may be concentrated in one month. Within the company this may be explained easily enough, but if the company is the subsidiary of a group it might cause eyebrows to be raised at headquarters. Accountants and marketors in the subsidiary company can in such circumstances work together to smooth advertising costs over a period, rather than let them bunch into peak months.

Ironically, well-intentioned joint measures of this sort can end in grief all round if a watch is not kept on one of the essential features of advertising expense. This is the extent to which the company has been committed to costs not yet incurred. Exhibitions, for example, often need to be booked months in advance, as may major campaigns in journals. Not all these commitments can be cancelled at short notice thereafter. An advertising manager therefore has to keep careful note of everything he or she has booked, and of when payment for it will fall due. The marketing manager needs to review this frequently with an eye to the budget, and to discuss its implications with the chief accountant. The historical figures available to the accounts department often give no indication of what is to come. From experience it might be added that the marketing manager needs to take positive steps to avoid unpleasant surprises where advertising is concerned. Accounts clerks have a tendency to classify any awkward expense as 'advertising', and the only way to prevent this is to put strict limits on the number of people allowed to authorize advertising expenditure.

The guardians of morality

When there is a sales force it can be much more difficult to reach an accommodation with accountants. However clearly they may come to understand the thinking behind marketing decisions, they are still likely to view the actions of sales people with suspicion. The direct connection between sales activity and orders received is not at all obvious to them. It is after all indisputable that if a company fired all its sales staff, orders would still come in. The only points at issue are how many and for how long. The accountant may have different answers from those the sales manager would give, and feel that the contribution made by sales representatives is often overstated, especially where commission is involved. It is quite possible for accountants to see the 'typical sales representative' driving around the country in a company car, running up an unjustified expense account and doing his or her best selling in the office, not in front of the customer.

I once knew an accountant who had a table tennis table in his garage. No one had ever seen him playing table tennis. The purpose of the table was far from that. What he did was to take home the expense claims of certain members of the sales force. He took a special interest in receipts for meals taken in the course of travelling. If any of the receipts looked similar to others, he would set them out on his table and study the numbers printed on them and the dates entered. Where numbers were sequential or very close to each other, he would investigate further, suspecting, sometimes correctly, that a given salesman had obtained an expense pad and was writing his own receipts.

Of course I could hardly complain of such devotion to duty. At the least it served to rid the company of some of the more stupid sales people we had made the mistake of employing. But zealotry in a righteous cause is a hard force to contain. Accountants were soon consulting large scale road atlases and stretching carefully measured pieces of string along all routes from A to B. This was to check mileage claims and raise queries when they did not represent the shortest possible route. As it turned out this was not so fruitful a field of research, if only because even sales representatives can sometimes get lost. So an 'incorrect mileage claim' never became a hanging offence.

The serious point for me was that by then it was generally believed that the accountants would like to have made it almost literally that. All sales people were seen as guilty until proved innocent, and innocent only until they were caught. I began to understand how a medieval bishop might have felt when the Inquisition took too keen an interest in his diocese.

Once relationships between the sales force and those enthusiastic guardians of the company's morality had fallen into this pattern, things which, for the majority at any rate, had been matters of conscience, became moves in a game. Sales representatives whose minds would have been better bent on obtaining business were spending more and more time discovering ingenious ways of justifying their expenses. It is one of the sadder facts of life that people who are repeatedly invested with a certain persona, whether it be well founded or not, and however unwelcome it may be at first, can eventually be pushed into acting the part they have been given.

There followed from this a risk that the conflict between sales representatives and accountants would spread to other levels of management. Local sales managers wanted to foster team spirit and to maintain discipline in their own way, not at the dictate of accounts clerks in head office. There was a natural clash of management style, which I could not resolve fully until a new generation of management accountants had taken over.

It is important to reach an understanding with accountants on issues of this kind. They have to exercise vigilance and are bound to bring the facts they discover to the attention of others. But outside the accounts department it is not for them to impose discipline. They are not the guardians of morality. Each individual is the guardian of his or her own morality. It seems at least possible that if the majority of people are encouraged to value their honesty, there will be fewer cheats to punish.

Joint involvement

Although it may be easier to work with accountants at the strategic level of business plans and annual budgets, joint involvement on tactical issues can be fostered in a number of ways. The control of advertising expenditure has already been discussed, and it will have been observed that in this, as on the strategic plane, the key is openness, giving more information than may be strictly needed to prepare any one month's figures and explaining just what it is that Marketing is trying to accomplish. The same principle applies elsewhere, including matters relating to the sales force. Shortly we shall be looking at ways in which Accounts may be involved in operating a commission scheme, but first it is worth considering how management accounts can act as a marketing tool.

Management accounts

Every company, large or small, relies for its day-by-day, or month-by-month operations on workman-like management accounts. If, as may perhaps be found in some small firms, they do not yet exist, it would be better to sit down and create some than to go on taking orders that may or may not turn out to be profitable. Marketing managers who cannot accept this, or who pay no attention to the detailed figures produced, are like craftsmen who do not read the drawings before picking up the tools.

A dialogue with the accounts department on what is or is not included under every heading in each set of figures as it appears is essential to an understanding of the business. So a marketing manager who has difficulty in interpreting income and expenditure accounts or who cannot explain any variance against budget, would be advised to spend some time with an accountant learning how. In an age of microcomputers there should be no shortage of figures for consideration and there is simply no place for innumerate managers.

If we can take this first stage for granted, the way is open to extend the use of management accounts as a marketing tool. There are no fixed rules about what is or is not to be included in the figures produced. Sales can be analysed by product, by market, by category of business, by type of customer, by region, or by anything at all that can be recorded when an order is taken, and which is of significance. Because of the need to make comparisons with past performance, the sooner categories for analysis are decided the better.

The importance of analysing the profitability of different products in the range has already been discussed. It may not always be easy to allocate overheads to individual product lines, but at least the analysis can go to gross profit level. It should be possible to go further in looking at branch or regional performance although the allocation of head office costs (for example, a proportion of the main advertising expense) may take some thought.

So far this assumes that confirmed sales orders or possibly invoices will be used as a basis for figures produced. Orders are preferable if there is any significant time between order and delivery, because management accounts need the most up-to-date information possible if they are to function as a guide to immediate action. There are however other sources of information, some of which normally fall outside the orbit of the accounts department, which might benefit from analysis.

Statistics about sales representatives' performance, about enquiries or about the conversion of enquiries to orders come into this category. They could be analysed entirely within the marketing department or the help of Accounts could be sought. As there are no rules about this, the decision will depend on the paperwork systems currently in operation, on staffing and on a perception of where the work will be more knowledgeably handled. If any payments are involved, Accounts would seem to be the obvious choice, but it should be remembered that statistics are only as good as the data on which they are based. If these are in any way vague or in need of interpretation – for example, of what is or is not an enquiry – all the work is better done within the department most familiar with the concepts used.

Operating a commission scheme

Where sales representatives are paid a commission both Accounts and Marketing are likely to be concerned with at least some aspects. Money has to be paid out, so it is inevitable that the payroll department will be involved. Yet because commission schemes are intended to provide an incentive to greater sales, it is likely that Marketing will take a leading part in their design. Between these points any number of arrangements can be made for managing a scheme effectively. For example, Marketing could operate the entire programme, simply letting the payroll department know what to pay, while at the other extreme the whole scheme could be run by Accounts once it has been set up.

My own experience indicates that benefit can be gained from making this a joint exercise. Just because of the stock attitudes with which accountants and sales people may regard each other, a scheme which runs smoothly through the combined efforts of Marketing and Accounts can do something to cement relations within the organization, while at the strategic level both departments will need to agree that the scheme is, and remains, within the broad objectives of the company as a whole. By inference all this implies that a scheme which is to be operated by the accounts department should be drawn up with the full knowledge and approval of those who will have to make it work. There is no point in a marketing manager designing something which creates more problems than it solves.

Designing the scheme

Commission schemes tend to start as something simple and become more and more complex as ways have to be found of dealing with the various situations and anomalies that arise. The hardest part of the initial design is to foresee as much of this as possible in advance. A badly drawn scheme, or one that needs frequent and major changes to keep sales effort in line with company objectives, is not likely to inspire sales people. Yet it is difficult to predict what will happen when you have laid out a set of rules specifically intended to alter behaviour. To the extent that you yourself have moved the goalposts, you should not be surprised when the ball comes from an unexpected direction.

When I first faced the problems of creating a new and workable scheme my company had a sales force of what might be called middling size, which grew to number 150. The range of products was already fairly wide, and diversification projects were to widen it still further. The questions which had to be addressed at the outset included:

- What was the amount of business expected from each sales representative?
- What remuneration were we prepared to pay for that amount of business?
- What variations around this figure did we anticipate?
- What proportion of average remuneration should be basic salary and what commission?
- Was the scheme to be open-ended or were limits to be placed on the commission that could be earned?

- Were we prepared to let a sales representative earn more than his or her immediate supervisor? Or more than senior managers?
- Were we going to pay an equal rate for all products and for all categories of business?
- If not, what differentials would be likely to serve the pattern of business required?
- Would we pay on booked or invoiced sales?
- If on booked (a more immediate reward for effort) what would we do if an order were subsequently cancelled?
- Would we pay on orders taken:

  –by individual sales representatives

  –on defined territories

  –from named customers?
- If payment were territory-based, how would we deal with:

  –exceptionally large customers?

  –national customers, with centralized buying?
- What flexibility, if any, should be given to local managers?
- Who should operate the scheme?
- How would disputes be settled?
- What appeals procedure should be applied?

There were in fact even more questions than these, since our business was taken partly via outright sale and partly via rental contracts of varying lengths. But the list given will serve as a sample of what had to be discussed in detail between Marketing and Accounts, and of course approved by the chief executive.

Day-to-day running of the scheme

The precise answers we arrived at have no prescriptive value now, and in any case, the scheme underwent several modifications over the years it was in force. Very briefly, it was a territory-based scheme, related to booked sales, and its detailed working was placed in the hands of a young management accountant. The accounts department had the staff to provide adequate back-up, but this one person dealt with all commission matters, interpreted the rules as they had been written and answered any queries from sales representatives or their supervisors.

At the end of each month a small batch of queries would remain on which he felt the need of a second opinion. Then he and I would sit down and decide what was permissible within the scheme and whether any exceptions should be made where entitlement to commission was a matter not of right, but of natural justice. After a while he became expert in all aspects of the scheme. From time to time minor changes to the rules were made to cater for problems that he or I had identified.

Exceptions and appeals

One of the more difficult aspects of a territory-based scheme is ensuring fairness in allocating territories. Past figures of sales in each area are too dependent on the level of manning achieved and on the quality of previous representatives. We used a combination of published statistics and local knowledge to estimate the relative potential of the 'bricks' that went to make up each representative's territory, and then made sure that area managers obtained the agreement of all concerned. In the rare event of a dispute I was prepared to arbitrate.

Most disputes however were not about territories, or between sales people and local management. They were between individual sales representatives, and about sharing commission. The problem was that a large customer might have a buying office in one representative's territory, but negotiations and the final installation could take place in another area altogether. As customers' buying practices varied it was sometimes not obvious where the decision to buy was really made. So each of two sales people could claim, and might genuinely believe, that the order was the direct result of his efforts. Naturally we had rules to deal with situations of this kind which normally worked, if in a somewhat arbitrary manner. Sometimes this was not enough to satisfy 'felt-fair' needs, and we were faced with two salesmen, each backed by his local manager, each claiming the commission on a given order. In the middle of such a dispute stood the management accountant, gaining a deep insight into the character and motivation of individual representatives and interpreting the rules as impartially as he could.

When he had to call on me to adjudicate, we examined together all possible precedents and looked at the likely consequences of decisions in either direction. Every decision I, as the ultimate arbiter, made was recorded in writing with reasons given, so that a body of 'case-law' was built up. Often the management accountant was able to handle problems on his own by reference to the rules and past decisions. He soon gained a reputation for fair dealing which did much to improve the inherently difficult relationship between Marketing and Accounts. On his part he acquired knowledge of the sales force as a collection of individuals not all of whom resembled the caricature of a typical sales representative we looked at earlier, any more than he was a 'typical accountant'.

As an exercise in joint involvement the commission scheme was a success, but a fair amount of management energy was absorbed in seeing that it ran smoothly. It could be argued that this might have been avoided by remunerating sales people in a different way without a commission element. This touches on broader issues which will be discussed in Chapter 4. To do so in this instance would have been difficult because the idea of commission was deeply entrenched and in its absence a major overhaul of intermediate management would have been needed to ensure that a high level of motivation remained. In a small company, or in a larger one where the choice is still open, it could be worth trying. It would however continue to be necessary to measure carefully the work of sales people and the results stemming from their efforts. For this I would be delighted to have that management accountant working by my side.

Small firms

The examples chosen for this chapter have been taken from experience in a sizeable company, which was a member of a large group where accounting discipline was strict. The relationship between Accounts and Marketing is no less important in smaller firms. In one sense it is easier to get it right, because problems of distance are less likely, and any attitude that needs redirection will be visible and comparatively accessible. But the integration of management effort is not that easy in any company. In small firms the problem may be that neither the people responsible for accounts nor those in charge of marketing are aware of the possibilities open to them.

Many small firms have yet to appreciate the value of detailed management accounts, whether for measuring costs, for analysing sales, or for assessing the relative profitability of different products.

What is needed then is someone with an analytical approach to see what is actually happening and to build up the regular returns and exhibits that will enable future progress to be measured. It does not matter much what 'hat' he or she is currently wearing. It could be that of the marketing manager, or of the accountant or of the chief executive. But someone has to be well enough informed to know what figures are required and to see that they are obtained.

The reason why it is hard to run a small business well is that to do so requires all the qualities that are needed to run a larger business, but concentrated into fewer individuals. The advantage is that if these qualities exist anywhere in the company, the task of harnessing them to present an integrated approach to marketing is much easier.

Questions and action points for decision takers

Assessing attitudes

What opinions do departmental heads hold of the accounts department?

How do your accountants regard the marketing department?

Strategic planning

Who is responsible for drafting long term business plans?

Do Marketing and Accounts work together on this?

What methods does Marketing use to forecast future sales?

Do they include estimates of:

- market potential
- penetration to date
- the trend of annual sales
- the shares of competitors
- overall economic trends
- legislative requirements or regulations
- threats from alternative technology
- the effect of additional promotion?

Have these factors been explained to colleagues, including Accounts?

Is there respect for the expertise of Marketing in this field?

Who makes decisions on long or short term choices?

Do accountants assist in drawing up alternative projections?

Trouble shooting

When sales do not run to forecast, what analysis is made?

Is information readily available on:

- customers so far obtained
- outstanding quotations

- prospective customers
- enquiry rate
- advertising programme and response time
- length of selling cycle
- sales activity
- sales performance of teams/individuals?

Has this been explained to and discussed by heads of all departments?

Sales expenses

How is the advertising expense handled in monthly accounts?

What record is kept of expenditure committed in advance?

How do your accountants regard salesmen and saleswomen?

How do sales people regard accountants?

Who is responsible for discipline over sales expenses?

Commission schemes

Is there a commission scheme?

Are its aims and likely consequences in line with company objectives?

Who operates it on a day-to-day basis?

Could Accounts do more?

Who authorizes exceptions and hears appeals?

Are all decisions recorded, along with reasons?

Management accounts

How detailed are management accounts?

Are sales analysed by:

- product
- market
- category of business
- type of customer

- sales representative
- region?

What else would help Marketing in making decisions?

Small firms

If a small firm:

- Who analyses and records essential sales data?
- Is it done regularly?
- What use does Marketing make of the figures provided?

4

Cutting the cackle

The sales force in perspective

So far we have been looking at the problems of integrating marketing activity with the efforts of other, non-marketing departments. Divergent views of the importance of the role played by each major department have been scrutinized, latent clashes of interest identified, and suggestions made which are aimed at a reshaping of attitudes. In doing this it has been necessary to refer to specific marketing functions, such as product management, selling or advertising, since some of the difficulties, and some of their remedies, are associated with only one aspect of marketing, rather than with marketing in its broadest sense.

That this should be the case indicates the possibility of another set of problems. These relate not simply to the integration of marketing into the fabric of the company as a whole, but to the integration of the marketing functions themselves. Divergences of interest between those engaged in advertising, public relations, selling or marketing planning may not be so obvious as those, for example, between Marketing and Production, but they can and do exist. Use of the term 'marketing mix' does not imply that the part to be played by each section of the marketing department has been studied in depth; even less that it has the agreement of all 'mixees'. Often it is just the employment of jargon to paper over time-honoured differences.

It seems historically correct to start with the sales force. Selling had its place in business for thousands of years before the word marketing was invented. Even after that, there was a brief period when for many marketing was just a longer word for sales. While it now seems generally accepted that the term does embrace functions other than selling, these are often seen as 'tacked on' to the sales operation. Sometimes the sales department remains organizationally distinct from anything called marketing. Even where there is a marketing manager in charge overall the sales force may still be pursuing its own way, regardless of what is being done in marketing planning or in advertising. Where marketing has been grafted on to an existing sales organization, in the form of additional bits of activity, it is unlikely that there will have been any radical rethinking or substantial changes in behaviour.

A problem of inheritance

In some firms it appears as if the place of the sales force has been decided by history rather than by deliberate choice. It was there from the beginning, along with the factory and the accounts department. Over the years it may have grown or shrunk in accordance with economic trends or success and failure in the market-place, but it is rare that its very existence will have been called into question. The process of obtaining orders has, after all, as fair a claim as any to being close to the heart of a business. So people with the job of meeting prospective customers face to face are unlikely to see other forms of marketing activity as anything more than ancillary. Least of all are they likely to see themselves as one means only of securing marketing objectives, and one which requires justification in the light of possible alternatives.

Sales attitudes

The attitude that sales representatives may display towards other departments has already received some attention. It is now time to summarize the way in which Sales may interact with departments outside Marketing, and to look more closely at the motivation involved. Then we will be in a better position to see how the sales force is likely to behave within the orbit of Marketing, and to see how matters may be improved.

Sales people stand directly in line between a company and its customers. Because of this, even in a sales force highly geared to a commission incentive, motives may be complex. People who are sensitive to the needs of customers will try to obtain from the company whatever it is their particular customers want. Of course they will also be trying to obtain orders for the company, but they may feel that the route to this lies through meeting specific requirements as closely as possible. If they do not speak up on the customer's behalf, who will? Persuasion therefore can work both ways; although it seems sometimes to be left in the car park when a sales representative returns to base, to be replaced by peremptory demands.

Even the best of intentions can create problems. To illustrate this let us invent two representatives to embody the extremes with which others may be faced, Joe Greed and Doris Goodly. Joe Greed has no doubt where his loyalty lies. He has all the qualities which feature in the more crass advertisements for sales personnel, ambition, drive, motivation and so on. He wants to top the sales lists, and to line his pockets with as much commission as he can lay his hands on. Doris Goodly shows much more empathy with her customers. She is sensitive to their demands and can be persistent in her efforts to obtain what is required.

Relations with Production, Development and Accounts

The factory has had problems with Joe, because of delivery promises made to snatch orders from competitors. Doris has, albeit reluctantly, kept within the rules set for delivery, but has obtained a number of orders which have entailed modifications to the standard product. Some of these have proved expensive. Joe's orders are often short on detail, so that both Production and Installation have had a number of arguments with him and with his customers about what is needed and when. Doris's paperwork has been meticulous, but the discussions she has had with customers after an order has been obtained, and even while installation is in progress, have raised a number of queries, caused some last minute changes and resulted in delays in payment.

At the annual sales conference various suggestions have been made for improvements to the product range. Joe is reasonably happy with the present designs, but insists that to meet competition, and beat it every time, price has to be reduced. No reduction in quality is acceptable however, and all the present features have to be maintained. Doris is also concerned about price, because some of her customers have told her that competitors are now making better offers, but what she would like to see is a number of new features that would meet objections raised on recent calls. Faced with a number of incompatible requests the development engineer is inclined to proceed on the line already proposed by his technicians.

Accounts have no complaints about Doris Goodly's expense claims. Joe Greed's expenses are another matter altogether, but when the accountants complain of this to his sales manager, they are told:

'Alright, so his expenses are high, but so are his sales!' The sales manager finds it a little harder to brush aside the arguments over commission associated with Joe. Here is a salesman who wishes to share neither reward nor credit for any order in which he claims to have had a hand. The management accountant anticipates problems from this direction, but is also concerned about one aspect of Doris Goodly's work. Orders taken cover a wide spread of profitability, but some of hers seem among the worst.

Relations within the marketing department

In the purely fictional situation we have created, Doris and Joe may be imagined to be members of a unified marketing department, incorporating market research, advertising, public relations and marketing planning. The people responsible for these activities are their colleagues. Apart from the problems of geographical separation, relations with them should be a good deal easier than is the case with people outside Marketing. That this is not always so may puzzle those with unquestioning faith in organization charts, but not others. A place on the branches of a common tree reporting upwards to a single chief is no guarantee of harmony. In favourable circumstances it may facilitate the settlement of disputes, but it will not stop them arising, or simmering beneath the surface.

Advertising and sales literature

Perceptions of the relative importance of Sales and Advertising cover a wide spectrum. In companies marketing consumer goods the main thrust of stimulating demand may fall on the advertising department, and sales representatives can then become shelf fillers and order collectors. We are however concerned primarily with industrial or business-to-business marketing. Here, for reasons which will shortly be discussed, the part played by sales people tends to be more important and the scope for advertising more limited.

There are still ample grounds for variation. As an example, salesmen like Joe Greed may do their own prospecting for potential customers or, as is sometimes the case where markets are widespread and prospects difficult to locate, advertising, direct mail or a tele-sales team could be used to identify places worth a call. From the point of view of sales representatives this is a matter of degree only. They are the front line troops: all else is support.

The problem is that there is no limit to the amount of support sales people would like, while there are sure to be limits to the funds available. Furthermore different representatives will have different ideas of the support that is needed. Joe Greed has noticed that locally based competitors are advertising in the *Yellow Pages* directories covering his area. He would like advertisements for every product in his range to be placed in the appropriate section of all *Yellow Pages* directories on or adjacent to his territory. Doris Goodly is more inclined towards advertising campaigns in local newspapers. She would not wish this to be at the expense of current advertising in trade journals and the national press, and is sympathetic to Joe's views on *Yellow Pages*. The advertising manager on the other hand feels that every penny is needed for his main national campaign if it is to have any real impact.

There has been some discussion among sales representatives on the effectiveness of the company's literature. Joe is satisfied with the present format which is applied to a series of leaflets covering each product individually, while Doris has been impressed by her major competitor's latest brochure, which contains information on the entire product range and has been given a glossy and authoritative finish. Both want literature to match and surpass anything that competition has to offer. Arguments about possible changes to the existing format tend to be unproductive however and the advertising manager believes that sales people in general are quicker to criticize than to suggest viable alternatives.

PR and exhibitions

PR is interpreted by both Joe and Doris as editorial coverage, and as such is welcomed, although it might be more accurate to say that they resent seeing competitors and competitive products featured in the press rather more strongly than they appreciate mention of their own company. At any rate when asked to suggest customers who could be the subject of an article, they both tend to become silent. For Joe this could lead to unproductive work when he could be out gathering fresh business. Doris sees a risk that the careful relationship she has built with her favourite customers could be damaged through the intervention of third parties, or even by the mere request for publicity.

Exhibitions may also produce ambivalent attitudes. National exhibitions provide an opportunity to meet other representatives and a change of routine. Talk of the company dropping out of its regular place in the annual trade show can produce dismay. Will our customers think we are no longer seriously in business? On the other hand both Joe and Doris know of local exhibitions that might assist sales on their respective territories. But when it is suggested that to make these effective they should canvass prospective customers to ensure that they attend, enthusiasm tends to wane.

Product policy and pricing

With a wide range of products at their disposal it is not surprising that our specimen representatives favour different items. Joe puts his effort into selling the simpler, straightforward offerings, although always with an eye to the possibility of multiple orders from his larger customers. Doris specializes in more complicated applications. Neither sells consistently across the range, but few members of the sales force do. The marketing manager has considered tweaks to the commission system to remedy this situation, but has fought shy of anything too drastic. Other aspects of product discipline have produced some strain, with requests for specials coming more frequently from Doris than from Joe. But when it comes to price cutting or allowing extra discount, Joe is the prime culprit.

Now I have never met Joe, although I have known a few salesmen like him. At one stage in my career I was amazed to discover just how many Joes there were in industrial selling. It is after all not an inquiry one would imagine to be susceptible to statistical method.

At the time, Bryan Atkin and I were conducting a survey which led to the publication of *How British Industry Prices*.[1] During the process I came across an odd finding. Of the companies questioned (220 in all) 41 per cent believed their prices were higher than average for their industry, 48 per cent thought they were about average, and only 7 per cent said theirs were lower than average (4 per cent did not answer this particular question). On the face of it, it seemed unlikely that 89 per cent of prices were in fact average or higher than average and only 7 per cent below average, but that is what people believed.

A clue to this enigma was provided by the answers to another question in the survey. It appeared that most of the companies which consciously looked at market price levels relied for their

[1] Atkin, B. and R.N. Skinner (1975), *How British Industry Prices*, Industrial Market Research Ltd., London.

information about competitors' prices on members of the sales force. It seems reasonable to assume that the general conclusion that most products are overpriced, or certainly not underpriced relative to competition, was influenced by sales representatives and their departmental managers.

The hand of Joe is clearly in this, but he should not take all the blame. It is more than possible that he and Doris and many others have been misled by their customers. In seeking a bargain it may well happen that a customer exaggerates the price advantages a competitor holds, and is less than meticulous in comparing like with like. Should the business finally be placed elsewhere the customer may again let a losing salesman understand that the decision has been made on grounds of price, rather than explain that it was because of the salesman's attitude, or lack of product knowledge or because of his company's poor reputation. Nevertheless once Joe believes that his prices really are too high he will try to persuade his company that this is true. If there are no other ways of checking the information provided, a good deal of unnecessary worry may ensue.

Where commission is paid the tendency to look for lower prices and to quote them wherever possible is amplified. If the price is reduced by 5 per cent, Joe still gets 95 per cent of what he would have received, rather than nothing.

The intention in listing the points at which tension can and does arise between members of the sales force and other people in the marketing organization is not to imply that these problems are incurable. They can be treated with every chance of success, but not just by tinkering with the organization chart. Some more radical thinking and more personal involvement is required.

The measures to be taken include:

1 Reassessment of the need for a sales force and of the role it has to play.

2 Realignment of its objectives with those of Marketing as a whole.

3 Consideration of alternatives to commission and of other measurements of sales effort.

4 Appraisal of ways and means of integrating field selling with other marketing activity.

5 Consideration of methods a marketing manager may employ to stay in touch with the thinking of the sales force.

Do you need a sales force?

Once I looked at the operations of a company serving the construction industry. It had five representatives who were all paid commission on orders received from clearly defined territories. The orders came from building contractors and the representatives would take measurements on site to ensure that the product would be installed correctly. There was no doubt that this was a valuable service or that the product deserved its large and enduring share of its particular market sector.

What I came to realize was that in almost every case orders came from enquiries sent direct to a central sales office. Quotations were then despatched and buying decisions made, either on grounds of value for money, or because the company had been specified by the architect involved. If additional information was required before a decision could be made, it was usually supplied over the telephone or facsimile network. On rare occasions sales representatives became involved, but they seldom met the architects, who had the greatest influence on purchasing. There was therefore no case for paying them commission, or indeed for employing them as anything other than measurers or site liaison staff. Nevertheless they had existed from day one and were considered inviolable.

It seems that what had happened in this instance was that a sales force which had some meaning when the product was a new idea had become virtually irrelevant once the company had achieved widespread acceptance. Changes in the market had not been mirrored in the company's sales structure or in its thinking about the relationship between buyer and seller.

Buyclasses

If we are to ask whether a sales force is necessary and if so, what sort of sales force we should have, it pays to turn the question upside-down and look not at selling, but at buying. It is all too easy in marketing to see customers as people we sell to. They however see themselves as people who *buy*, not as passive 'sellees'. A study of the buying process therefore helps to indicate the kind of selling that is appropriate.

As far as I know this idea was first developed systematically by Robinson, Faris and Wind.[2] The authors distinguished three different types of buying situation:

- the straight rebuy
- the modified rebuy
- the new task

Every purchase falls into one or other of these categories.

A manufacturer buying raw materials, a retailer restocking his or her shelves, or a chief draughtsman purchasing pencils and draughting film are all performing the task of a *straight rebuy*. What they purchase is defined in advance and no changes are required. They will of course want to see quality maintained, and could have queries on delivery or price, but apart from that their need for information is strictly limited.

In a *modified rebuy* there are significant changes. At one time the chief draughtsman was buying not film but transparent tracing paper. The move to polyester film to accomplish the same task as paper was not lightly undertaken. The buyer had to think about more than price and delivery. In a modified rebuy the fitness of the product for its intended purpose is paramount. So more information is needed and more assurance that the modified product will do its job. Nevertheless the overall requirement is a familiar one, as is the use to which the product will be put.

With a completely new buying task, which for the sake of verbal consistency I will call a *new buy*, the purchaser is treading on unfamiliar ground. Suppose that the manager of a drawing office is not ordering supplies, but contemplating a change to computer-aided design. This involves more than a choice between the various makes of equipment available, none of which is, in any case, familiar. The whole operation of the drawing office is going to be altered. Information is needed on all that this will bring in its train. Will fewer draughtsmen be required? How will they operate? What seating and lighting arrangements will be needed? Will the software enable parts lists to be produced simultaneously with drawings? Have numbering schemes to be revised? Who will do this? How will staff be trained to use the new equipment? The full list of queries is quite long enough before it reaches the final choice of software and

---

[2]Robinson, P.J., C.W. Faris and Y. Wind (1967), *Industrial Buying and Creative Marketing*. Allyn and Bacon Inc., Boston.

hardware. Compared with a straight or modified rebuy there is a need for much more information on the application of the product to its task and about the alternatives available.

What a sales representative is for

Customers have a number of ways of obtaining information before making buying decisions. Advertisements, catalogues, samples and the opinions of existing users can all contribute something. In the case of a straight rebuy or in some of the simpler modified rebuys those sources might be sufficient in themselves, perhaps with the addition of a telephone call to check price and delivery.

With a complex modified rebuy or a new buy more questions have to be asked, and neither the written information available nor what can be obtained by telephone may be enough. Queries have to be raised, the answers given studied carefully and supplementary questions put when necessary. So the potential buyer needs to talk to someone knowledgeable. Whether this is a sales representative or an engineer or the managing director of the supplying company does not usually matter so long as all the questions raised can be answered in a satisfactory way. Salesmen and saleswomen, seen from this point of view, are simply sources of information.

From this it follows that if no new or detailed information is required before a decision is made, the customer may see no need to talk to anyone on the sales side of a company. In our earlier example of a company serving the construction industry, what had been a modified rebuy, a new way to supply an established need, had become something more like a straight rebuy. The majority of orders could be handled by well-trained clerks in the sales office. The company had itself brought about this situation, by its success in the market and by issuing architects with catalogues which made it easier to specify the product. A case could possibly have been made out for employing one or two field representatives to handle the larger or more complex enquiries, but not without investigating just how much information the customer needed in these instances.

The other side of the coin

When selling is looked at from the buyer's point of view it appears as an honourable craft, and an essential element in a wide range of transactions. If salesmen and saleswomen did not already exist, they would have to be invented. Yet it is the company which employs them that has to foot the bill, and it is not paying them merely to provide potential customers with the information they need. An estimate of how much information is required will indicate whether a sales force is necessary and what its members will have to know in order to talk to customers with authority. It may also suggest how large a part could be played by alternative methods of marketing which do not involve face-to-face selling. But the final size and shape of the sales force and the exact constitution of the marketing mix of which it forms a part will involve consideration of the company's interests at least as much as those of its customers.

Factors which need to be reviewed include:

- whether the company is attacking or defending a market
- whether the value of each order justifies direct selling
- how easy it is to locate prospects
- what alternative marketing tactics could be applied

Attack or defence?

It will be clear from what has been said so far that a company already enjoying a large share of a given market would like to ensure that its customers go on treating each order as a straight rebuy. It follows that a company trying to attack such a market will attempt to turn what has up to now been a straight rebuy into a modified rebuy. This might be done simply by offering a similar product at a lower price, or it might be done by offering a more attractive product. If the latter course is chosen the difference between products and the advantage claimed by the attacker may need explanation. There would therefore be a role for a well-briefed and hard-hitting sales force.

Defence could take several forms. Some companies employ sales people to keep in touch with existing customers and give them reassurance that their present buying policy is correct. Against a determined attack backed by a product with apparent advantages this is likely at best to win a little time. Certainly assurance is something a sales representative can give, but a buyer is more impressed by fresh, factual information. It might therefore be more economic to reduce prices rather than employ sales people in a purely defensive role.

What is more likely is that the defending company will itself make modifications to its product, so that both it and its attacker are offering modified rebuys. This may in turn reinstate a part for the sales force to play. The possibilities of compromise solutions exist at every stage. For example, if the defending company has a number of exceptionally large customers it might keep personal contact with them, while adopting other tactics elsewhere. While an attacker, using price as the main weapon, might still try direct selling to such large and lucrative targets.

The value of each order

It might seem that when a product is a genuine innovation there is a need for 'creative' selling, that would in any case necessitate a sales force to provide customers with information and to persuade them to make a completely new buy. Often this is true, but an eye has to be kept on the value of each order when selling direct to the end user. Selling-time costs money, and if the value of an order does not justify the time spent getting it, another way has to be found.

Often markets start with pioneering manufacturers selling direct to end users, then when the benefits of the product become more widely appreciated, and especially if the price falls as greater quantities are produced, the market shifts to dealers and distributors. This has happened in the market for office equipment and computers, for example. Some companies were slow to recognize the changes taking place and tried to continue to sell direct, when such an operation was no longer economic.

Locating prospects

Industrial markets may be small and well-defined, or widespread. A compact market makes it easy to gauge the size of sales force required, should all the other factors indicate that one is needed. A widespread market where the potential for a product is almost universal, could also be tackled economically if direct selling is applicable. What is difficult is a market where prospects are scattered and hard to locate, or one where buying decisions are made at infrequent intervals. In such cases it may still be feasible to use the sales force to track down likely buyers but only if the value of each order compensates for the time spent prospecting. It is often better to seek alternative ways of locating prospects, so that a sales representative can spend as much time as possible face to face with someone who could realistically be expected to place an order.

Alternative marketing tactics

Basic thinking about the need for a sales force and the sort of sales force that is appropriate starts from the customer's information requirement and takes in the company's stance in the market, the value each order will yield and the location of prospects. It should certainly include consideration of whether to sell direct to end users or via wholesalers, retail outlets or dealers. Policy needs to be reviewed at intervals frequent enough to allow for changes that may be taking place in the structure of the market. At each review the possibility of adjustments to the marketing mix can be considered.

Instead of sales people canvassing to locate prospects, advertising or direct mail might be used to bring the prospects to them. Experiments to see if alternative methods will work and prove economic are easy enough to stage. The same considerations apply to tele-sales or local exhibitions, or to supplying customers with catalogues.

A shift to selling via distributors or dealers is another matter altogether. Experiments may be possible in remote areas, but will usually prove inconclusive. It is a major strategic decision which is under consideration, not an adjustment to the current mix. To make such a decision a view has to be taken of the future market and of the nature and value of the products that will be offered by the participants in it.

Even when no changes are made after reviews of this kind, the result will be that the activity of the sales force will have been kept in line with the company's objectives and that its position as one element in a broader marketing mix will have been confirmed. That in itself will do a great deal to integrate its work with that of the rest of the marketing department.

Should commission be paid?

Payment by commission remains to be considered. In itself it serves to separate sales representatives from others in marketing and indeed from the rest of the company. Several of its less positive effects have already been outlined. The case in favour of it rests on its motivational value, especially where sales people have to find their own prospects and make cold approaches. There is no doubt that whether or not this can be described as 'hard' selling it is certainly hard work. It can also be dispiriting work on days when no one appears remotely interested in what a representative has to offer.

It is possible however to wonder whether commission acts as an incentive or as a disincentive on those bad days. There is no doubt that Joe Greed feels good when the orders are rolling in and he is contemplating a fat cheque at the end of the month. But when this is not the case the personal consequences of lack of orders can become very apparent.

Thoughtful marketing managers acknowledge this, at least implicitly, by putting emphasis on other, non-financial incentives. Team loyalty, pride in the company's products, or its service to customers, the development of craft skills (or professionalism, if it is wished to call it that), leadership and counselling, all come into play. Each of these implies a different approach to motivation from the 'carrot and stick' of commission schemes. People are not donkeys and do respond to other forms of persuasion. So could we not dispense with commission and rely entirely on the management techniques which are applied elsewhere in the organization?

The difficulty is that we seldom start from scratch. Abandoning commission and putting an existing sales force on to flat salaries is bound to be controversial and could prove expensive. Sales managers may also be worried by the apparent risk of feather-bedding non-producers. One of the benefits of commission is supposed to be that sales people who do not earn any tend to sack themselves. Experience however indicates that they do not always do so, or that they take too long over it. And in any case, what sort of thinking is it that removes from management the task of deciding who should stay and who should go?

In practice, given the will to manage, the elimination of poor performers is at least as easy in the sales department as elsewhere in the firm. Sales people are accustomed to measurement, and this can and should continue whether or not commission is paid. By extending measurement beyond a simple account of the value of orders received, greater fairness can be applied in assessing performance. The same techniques also help to improve performance by setting a number of smaller, achievable goals which lead progressively to more orders.

Measurement

Although business obtained must be the final criterion of success in selling, it is a comparatively crude yardstick when applied at any one time to any one sales representative. The 'top sales rep' in a company may not necessarily be the best, merely the luckiest over the period in question. One or two large orders can make all the difference between success and failure. Many companies therefore look at results in greater detail, and also at the effort that has gone in to producing the sales that have been obtained. From these figures a number of ratios are derived which point the way to improvement. As an example we could examine:

Results

- value of orders
- number of orders
- number of repeat orders (where appropriate)
- product mix
- product profitability (if sales people can influence this),

Effort

- number of approaches (by letter, telephone or in person)
- number of interviews (first or subsequent)
- number of demonstrations (by product, if appropriate)
- number of quotations (by product, first and revised quotes).

Ratios

- approaches : interviews
- interviews : demonstrations
- interviews : quotations
- demonstrations : orders
- quotations : orders.

In specific cases there will be many more facets of sales work that could be studied (e.g. type of customer, geographical area, etc.). No sales person is going to be equally good at all aspects of the job. The figures and ratios produced make it possible to identify the strengths and weaknesses of individuals and to follow this up with counselling and training.

More importantly, ratios provide each member of the sales force with a means of analysing his or her own selling skills, and of deciding whether the quicker way to success is to build on existing strengths or to try to eliminate any obvious weakness. A study of company-wide statistics will enable realistic goals to be set against which improvement can be measured.

It is necessary that techniques of this kind should be applied with a sensitive touch. There is no way in which everyone can be drilled into working to identical ratios. If any attempt is made to do this truthfulness and trust will suffer. However there is much to be gained from demystifying salesmanship and letting it be seen as a craft that can be mastered, rather than as a maverick activity, divorced from anything that happens elsewhere in the company.

Measurement can be employed whether or not commission is paid, but it does suggest that it may be possible to manage without commission. The difficulty of abandoning an existing scheme has already been mentioned, but new ventures may offer opportunities for fresh thinking, as may occasions when, for economic reasons, a major reorganization is inevitable.

Once the role of the sales force has been re-examined, to bring it into line with current marketing objectives, and a review made of the way in which sales people are motivated and led, the remaining steps towards integration are comparatively simple. We shall take a brief look at the relationship with other aspects of marketing, because these are covered more fully in later chapters, then touch on the ways a marketing manager has of communicating with the sales force and understanding its real problems.

Relationships within the marketing department

Advertising

It is natural enough to consult members of the sales force on advertising. They have to live with the results of it, and there is no monopoly of ideas. Gathering ideas is very different however from evaluating them or putting them into practice. Market research or internal analysis of the returns from advertising programmes or direct mail shots will give a more objective picture of how successful a campaign has been, and of the direction which subsequent efforts should take. Also the design of an advertisement or of a sales leaflet is something which seldom goes well if undertaken by a committee. It is inevitable that specialist skills must be used here, and that the role of the sales force can be only advisory.

What is important is that campaigns and promotional material should be designed with field selling in mind. It is not simply that advertisements and sales people should tell the same story, but that objectives should be set for every promotional item and that in setting them, the face-to-face selling that will follow should be fully considered. How, for example, will a leaflet be used in the course of a sales presentation? Is an advertisement designed to produce enquiries for representatives to pursue, or is it to provide a background awareness of the company and a favourable image?

When these matters are settled and a campaign prepared, communication with people in the field should be automatic. The only difficulties tend to revolve around dates. It is sometimes hard to get full details to representatives before the first insertion appears in the press, and any changes in the programme need to be notified as soon as possible.

Measuring the results of campaigns is another area which sometimes strains relations between sales staff and the advertising department. It is easiest in the case of direct mail where at least there can be a list of addresses mailed to compare with a list of orders received, but even so a mailing shot may have been sent to a customer with whom a sales representative was already in touch. In the case of advertisements it can be more difficult to trace an order back to its origin, especially where a long sales cycle is involved. Systems for doing this which rely on sales people completing forms are unlikely to yield accurate information, especially in companies which accord high prestige to orders obtained by 'cold calling'. Methods of assessing results will be discussed in Chapter 5. Here it may be said that they are better if designed to operate without imposing additional paperwork on sales staff, and that they may well have to provide approximate rather than accurate information, since in an industrial company with an extended selling cycle this may be all that is available. It may also be all that is necessary.

PR

It could seem a tautology to say that with PR it is communication that counts. But sometimes the communication is between a PR specialist and the company's managing director, not between PR and the sales force. The first step is to see that copies of all press cuttings are available to the sales staff. For many firms this is routine. The result should be to encourage representatives to find customers of their own who are not averse to publicity. Nevertheless most would rather be moving on to the next order than asking awkward questions of existing customers. Again paperwork systems are likely to prove futile.

What works is for the person responsible for PR to get to know every member of the sales staff. Once he or she is trusted to handle customers tactfully and efficiently, it will be possible to examine details of incoming orders and, if any fit the profile required for a press release, make direct contact with the representative concerned.

Exhibitions

Exhibitions will be considered in more detail later. Here we are concerned with the attitude of the sales force towards them. Much of the thinking of sales staff about the value of exhibitions and of the choice between local and national venues depends on the approach taken by management. Exhibitions cost money, absorb selling time and are very hard work for those manning the stand. If sales people think of them in any other way, for instance, as a welcome or even a boozy break from routine, or a chance to get together with colleagues rarely seen, there is something wrong with discipline.

At an exhibition all selling is done in public, in front of fellow representatives and managers as well as potential customers. The discipline in terms of attendance to the minute and deportment on the stand is altogether of a different order from that of the day-to-day sales job. There is no relaxation at all behind that welcoming smile. If this is understood and accepted by everyone then the sales representatives and their managers alike will be looking for a return on the work put in, and will be interested only in those exhibitions which bring results.

Assessing the results of an exhibition may take time. It is probably best to provide everyone with the information readily available, number and value of orders taken on the stand, number and profile of visitors and so on, and then to give a considered assessment later. It may take time to do this because some enquiries might not mature quickly, and it may not be possible to trace accurately the extent of business stemming from the exhibition alone. The company has however to make an estimate of this before committing resources to a similar exercise, and there is every reason to share the information with those who took part and those who might be called upon to do so in future.

Product policy

Something has already been said of the importance of product discipline. It is axiomatic that a firm grip must be kept on specials, delivery quotations and prices. In larger firms a product manager may be appointed to control these aspects. Suppose however that the range of products sold is wide. There may be more than one product manager responsible for various sections of it, and each will have a target for sales of products within his or her jurisdiction. If all products are channelled through a single, unified sales force how do we ensure that they are sold in the right proportion?

Tweaks to commission are seldom an effective answer to this sort of problem. If minor, their effect is likely to be short term, but if the balance is tipped too far, further corrective tweaks are needed *ad infinitum*. It is better to seek the cause of apparent discrepancies. Assuming that the potential for sales exists, the fact that some sales people are not meeting target for some products may be due to territorial anomalies, but is more likely to be the result of lack of confidence on the representative's part. Whether this is lack of confidence in the product or in an individual's ability to sell it, the first step is to reassess training needs.

When a company is diversifying and the product range is expanding rapidly, even the best training may leave some sales people favouring one part of the range and some another. An examination of the markets for all products might well indicate that an overall increase to the size of the sales force is feasible. There are two main approaches to this:

1 Make all territories smaller so that sales quotas can be achieved only by selling across the whole range.

2 Split the sales force into product divisions, so that each representative has fewer products to sell.

If the markets for all products are similar, or overlap to any extent, marketing theory would favour the first approach. Each customer is then served by only one representative, territories are more compact, and car mileage is reduced. Why then do so many companies go the other way in these circumstances, and divisionalize? One reason may be that sales people do not like having the size of their territories reduced. If this is to be done a good deal of persuasion and some convincing figure work will be required. For a deeper understanding of the attraction of the product division we need to go back to first principles.

What the customer wants is information. If a sales representative cannot supply this, even after extra training, because the product range is just too wide, he or she will not be successful, and next time may not even try. To be successful a representative needs not only theoretical knowledge but an established base of satisfied users for every product on offer. With too many items, it becomes hard to construct such a base in reasonable time. Specialists, on the other hand, rapidly become more experienced and better informed about what it is they have to sell.

The arguments about mileage still hold good, but with proper territory organization selling time in front of the customer will not be seriously curtailed, and will be put to much more effective use.

Other forms of communication

In addition to specific measures to communicate with the sales force about sales promotion and product policy, there are more general ways in which marketing managers may seek to integrate field representatives into the broad marketing aims of the company. The main difficulty in communication is the fact that selling is a lonely job. It is indeed an extreme example of the spatial separation looked at in Chapter 2. Of course there is no shortage of mechanical means of bridging the gap imposed by distance: anything from memos and newsletters to mobile telephones and computer terminals may be employed. But these are not going to be sufficient to ensure that sales people and marketing managers are acting in unison and with a clear understanding of the job each is trying to do.

Sales conferences

Sales conferences have been a traditional way of overcoming the problem of isolation, but it is possible to set too high a hope on what they can achieve. They may be a useful platform for launching major changes of policy, introducing new products, for example, or announcing a revised commission scheme, but large gatherings are rarely a genuine exercise in two-way communication, or seen as such by those participating. And without a theme of real substance they can soon degenerate into grousing sessions, either in the meeting or afterwards in the bar. A weak agenda provides opportunities for barrack room lawyers, which can be countered only by tight control from the chair, and that normally means a management harangue.

Although managers may find them more time-consuming smaller meetings, perhaps held locally, can allow real discussion to take place, and might seem preferable even when major issues are involved. Take, for instance, a new product launch. Holding a number of meetings with groups of representatives may well spread the launch over a week or two, rather than accomplishing it on one grand occasion, but it will enable genuine training to be provided, and a check to be made on the level of understanding achieved.

Field visits

When there is a sizeable sales force the marketing manager needs to be a good and discerning listener. He or she also needs to be accessible to all sales people, not simply to those who make the most noise. One of the ways to achieve this is to go out selling with them.

For many this will not seem a novel point to make. Is it not exactly what they did when there was that problem with customer A? Didn't they go along with the salesman and talk to the buyer to explain the company's position? Well, of course they did, and quite rightly so, but that is not what I have in mind. Special customers will always require special action, but by their very definition they are not typical of those with whom a sales representative spends the working day.

A field visit should mean accompanying a salesman or saleswoman throughout the whole of as near normal a day as possible. In this way a marketing manager comes to see the market from within, to hear what potential customers have to say, and to share the experiences of field sales staff. Few activities are more rewarding or more valuable when it comes to making decisions on policy, whether they involve the sales force or other sections of the marketing department.

In many firms it is quite normal for a sales representative to be accompanied on routine calls by his or her immediate supervisor. On-the-job training can hardly be handled in any other way. Yet even this essential part of a representative's development is often skimped, so that the supervisor is present only on 'important' calls or for part of the day. One reason for this is that it is not an easy role to play. To do it effectively the supervisor has to act in an anonymous fashion, to let the sales representative do the talking, and to reserve comment and advice until after the call. For someone more senior it may be harder still, and just as difficult to handle if the representative is to behave in a relaxed way.

There are rules to be followed if such an exercise is to be successful, and repeatable. An obvious one is that rank is irrelevant on the road. You are there simply as a colleague. If the customer believes that the representative is training you, so much the better. A second and more difficult rule to follow is that no one should suffer as a result of your visit. In other words, you are there to experience the market, not to report any failings back to your representative's supervisor.

From experience I would add a third rule, which is that it should be a *full* day. The reason for this is that you are not anonymous to the representative. Some showpiece calls may therefore be arranged, and some axe grinding can be expected. Very rarely does this last beyond mid-afternoon. Sometimes then there is a polite reminder that the traffic gets heavy about the rush hour, so if you want to get home in reasonable time .... The answer is always: 'Well, I'm here to spend the whole day with you, so where are we going next?' What is learnt in the subsequent hour or two may be worth all of the rest of the day. And if this technique does not work you can always make it two days rather than one.

After a few visits the sales force comes to accept the interest that has been shown in the selling job, and the integrity of the marketing manager where individuals are concerned. A channel of communication has then been opened which will enable better marketing decisions to be made. It will also, more than any form of words could, let sales people know they are not isolated but part of a unified marketing organization.

Questions and action points for decision takers

Sales attitudes

How long has the sales force existed?

How long is it since its role in marketing was seriously examined?

How do your sales people regard other parts of the company?

Have there been problems stemming from:

- desire for commission
- priorities demanded for particular customers
- optimistic delivery promises
- inflated sales expenses
- unprofitable orders?

What do your sales people think of the company's:

- advertising
- sales literature
- PR
- exhibitions
- product policy
- pricing policy?

The need for a sales force

What type of 'buy' are your customers making:

- straight rebuy
- modified rebuy
- new buy?

How do you assess their information requirement?

Does it justify face-to-face selling?

Are you attacking or defending a position in the market?

Have you considered alternatives to personal selling?

Does the value of each order justify direct selling?

Is it easy for sales people to locate prospects?

If not, are there alternative methods of doing this?

Alternatives to commission

Are sales representatives paid commission?

If so, have other methods of motivation been considered?

What measurement is applied to sales results:

- value of orders
- number of orders
- number of repeat orders
- product mix
- product profitability
- other factors?

How is sales effort recorded:

- number of approaches
- number of interviews
- number of demonstrations
- number of quotations
- other activity?

What ratios are studied:

- approaches : interviews
- interviews : demonstrations
- interviews : quotations
- demonstrations : orders
- quotations : orders
- others?

Are all these figures discussed regularly by sales representatives?

Are any targets set realistic?

Are they in line with wider company objectives?

Integrating sales promotion

Are advertisements and sales literature designed with field selling in mind?

Is the sales force kept fully informed on the timing of campaigns?

Does the person responsible for PR know each representative individually?

Do sales people accept exhibitions as serious selling exercises?

Are they informed of results?

Are representatives obtaining the correct product mix in orders?

If not, can extra training bridge any gap?

Is there a case for:

- smaller territories *or*
- a split into product divisions?

Communicating with the sales force

What objectives are set for sales conferences?

Will they be achieved, or would a series of smaller meetings be more effective?

When did you, or the marketing manager, last spend a full day accompanying a sales representative in the field?

5

Warp and woof
Integrating sales promotional activity

To the layman the word 'marketing' often conjures an image of slick promotional techniques designed to part consumers from their money. Sadly enough for many in industry too, the concept of marketing is limited to a view of advertising, PR, direct mail or exhibitions: as if the tools themselves defined the craft in which they are used. From here it is a short step to come to regard marketing as something that can be added on to an organization with no regard for existing attitudes or activities. And because outsiders, such as advertising agencies, are usually involved, what can be added can quite easily be deleted when it is seen to fail, as most likely it will.

These tools are however expensive and can waste a good deal of money in the hands of unskilled craftsmen. So we should look at them in turn to see where things can go wrong, and how it is possible to integrate specific promotional activities into the wider marketing aims of the company. In doing so it should be remembered that we will be concentrating on industrial or business to business marketing and thinking of medium- and small-sized firms as well as large. The relative importance of any particular promotional technique can be very different in these circumstances, compared with its standing in a major consumer organization.

Advertising

Consumer advertising can both promote a company's name and sell its product, or at least lay stress on what are seen as the main virtues of the product: for example, that it washes colours better or costs less. In industrial selling the message to be conveyed is often complex, which means that it cannot be carried by advertising alone.

The amount of information needed by customers may call for face-to-face selling, and for quite elaborate literature or other sales aids. The precise role of advertising may then be less clearly defined. The marketing budget also has to cover a range of promotional expenses, and if the company is small, a major part of the total may be devoted to sales literature, leaving press advertising with comparatively little.

The result of this is that an industrial advertiser may be a trifle vague about what can be expected to be achieved from the limited resources available. All too often the problem is then passed on to an advertising agency, without recognizing a potential clash of interests.

Although advertising agencies have expanded the scope of the services they offer, there is no doubt that they prefer to handle press or television advertising, rather than other forms of promotion. They get more income from it for every hour worked. An ambitious press campaign, based on two or three advertisements, may involve less design and copywriting than one good sales leaflet, but is much more lucrative.

There can therefore be a serious difference between what an advertising agent would like to provide and what is best for an industrial client. It is neither fair nor sensible to expect the agency to resolve this objectively, yet something of the sort is implied whenever an agency is approached with an imprecise brief and a request to: 'Tell us what you can do for our company.' From such a starting point the route to an advertising programme which is unrelated to the rest of the company's marketing effort is downhill all the way.

The agency approach

Agencies need new clients from time to time and are prepared to sell hard to get them. Naturally they prefer to sell to the chief executive if at all possible, and may demonstrate a high degree of skill in presenting their services to potential clients. What matters however is not the powers of persuasion directed at you, but the likely effectiveness of any promotion directed at your customers.

Good agencies will have found out as much as possible about the company and its markets before the presentation is made, but what can be discovered is strictly limited. There is no time for in-depth market research and in most cases it would cost too much, relative to the profit likely to accrue from handling the account. A few agencies have tried to sell a research package prior to an advertising presentation, but have found it hard to do.

What usually emerges can therefore be expected to feature press advertising, with a selection of journals based on an interpretation of readership statistics. Other services may of course be offered. In order to demonstrate a freshness of approach it is quite common to make a case for creating a new and improved image. Whether the funds are available to support the weight of advertising needed to achieve this is another question. If they are not, a compromise is likely to prove disappointing. Half a new image is not a viable concept.

Strangely enough, priority is often given to the company's logo. This can usually be guaranteed to receive the full attention of the chief executive, even if the logo is seen only by a handful of customers in a limited market who are otherwise fully aware of the company and what it offers. In this and in other ways the advertising 'pitch' at times appears to be modelled on presentations more appropriate to consumer accounts. Such presentations can however be effective if aimed at directors who believe that the first step in a promotional programme is to select an advertising agency to handle it.

Taking charge

It may be true that the selection of a competent agency is a necessary and important step in the process, but it is never the first step. If all forms of sales promotion are to be integrated with the efforts of the sales force and are to be consistent with the objectives of the company as a whole, this cannot be left to people outside the company. It is exactly what a marketing manager is paid to manage. Whether or not a new image is needed, for example, is something which should be known long before an agency is approached.

This is however only one aspect of a much wider range of questions which the company has to answer for itself. What resources are needed and how they should be deployed has to be settled, at least in outline, well in advance. Should money be spent on additional representatives or on direct mail, press advertising, literature or PR? The marketing manager cannot expect the suppliers of promotional services to make such decisions, although good ideas from outsiders might be allowed to influence the ultimate choice of media, or even the fine tuning of the budget.

The information on which the basic decisions about resource allocation can be made is readily available, or can be obtained by relatively simple forms of market research. With advertising, as with other elements in the marketing mix, it is normally a matter of setting clear objectives and measuring results. Once this is done on a regular basis it is possible to see what works and what does not. But before looking at the process in more detail it may be worth asking whether you need any press advertising at all.

If a market is small and compact, so that the potential buyers are known, it might be more effective to write to them all personally, or to call on them, than to place an advertisement in a journal they are supposed to read. This is of course an extreme example. The case for advertising becomes more cogent when potential customers are more widely scattered and difficult to locate. But there will be many intermediate points at which the question of cost-effectiveness can be raised, or where the alternative merits of direct mail or PR might be considered.

Advertising comes into its own when there is real difficulty in locating prospects, or when, as in the consumer field, prospects are so numerous that it is the most economical way of reaching them. In industrial selling potential customers may be scattered across time as well as geographically. This is because some purchases, of for example machine tools, or internal telephone systems, are made only when a clear need is discerned, and are not likely to be renewed or replaced for some years to come. In these circumstances advertising can bring your company to the notice of the unknown proportion of your market that is currently interested in the product you are offering.

Deciding objectives

In the last instance there is an assumption that, if you cannot easily get to your prospects, advertising will bring them to you instead. This implies that the objective is to obtain enquiries but there are other objectives that might be perfectly valid. A company attacking a new market may be unknown to potential buyers, or at least unknown in the context of the product now being offered. Consequently it may not be considered a credible source of supply. So even where prospects can be located and approached by other means, a case could be made for an advertising campaign to create awareness and pave the way for direct contact.

Advertising may also serve to build or reinforce the reputation of a company, or the image that it presents to its customers. In industrial selling it would be hard to make a case for it solely on these grounds. Reputations depend more on the product and on the service provided than on any slogan, no matter how apposite.

We have identified three possible objectives:

1 to create awareness of the company and its products

2 to reinforce a favourable image of the company

3 to obtain enquiries

But they are not mutually exclusive. If awareness is the prime objective, you are going to try to see that it is awareness of a *good* company. Likewise you are hardly likely to turn away any enquiries that come in as a result of an advertisement designed simply to promote the company's image. This in no way detracts from the importance of deciding what the main objective of a campaign is to be. By doing so the chances of success are enhanced and the yardstick against which success will be measured will have been determined in advance.

If the objective is increased awareness, it will be necessary to decide how the extent of any increase is to be judged. If it is enquiries that are wanted, machinery needs to be in place to count and evaluate the enquiries that follow. Setting clear objectives and assessing results against them are two sides of the same coin. Together they offer the greatest assurance that advertising will be an integral part of the marketing plan, and not a bolt-on extra.

Measurement

The propensity of advertising agents to recommend campaigns of so general a nature that it becomes difficult to measure success or failure is well known. It has some justification in so far as a campaign may produce results which are not immediate, but accrue over a period of time, making it harder to say what is due to advertising and what to extraneous factors. However it is no longer respectable to say that half the advertising budget is wasted, but which half is not known. It would now be more appropriate to say that if the result of a promotional effort cannot be measured, the money should be spent on something else.

The key to making such an approach practicable is to accept a certain degree of approximation in the measures applied. If we take awareness or, where awareness exists, the corporate image, there is no difficulty in finding where the company now stands, relative to its competitors. A simple and comparatively inexpensive market survey will establish this and serve as a bench mark for assessing changes following a campaign. Fine movements will not be detected in this way, because they will be within the range of normal statistical error, but if all your campaign has produced is fine movements it was probably a waste of time and money.

If the objective was to produce enquiries it will appear easier to measure results, but even here some difficulties may be encountered. It is necessary in comparing campaigns to identify not just the number of enquiries, but the type of enquiry produced. Are you looking for firm enquiries from people with a definite need in mind, or for enquiries from those interested just enough to seek further information? The objectives set should make this clear. Then you may have problems identifying enquiries stemming from specific advertisements, even if a coupon response is provided. People may write in without using the coupon, or telephone. It may be necessary to accept a fairly crude measurement of identifiable returns over a limited period, recognizing that this is not the whole story. If applied consistently it will enable comparisons to be made between campaigns or between individual advertisements.

The yellow telephone Fortunately it is sometimes possible to be very accurate indeed. At one time I had to deal with a sales team which appeared convinced that the only reason why results were not better was a failure on the part of the company to advertise more strongly in *Yellow Pages*. The belief in that particular branch was that national advertising had little effect locally. Businessmen in those parts were not sophisticated, and their requirement for any of our products was by nature spasmodic. So it was only natural for them to consult *Yellow Pages* when a need became apparent.

There was of course no reason to reject this argument out of hand. The consequences of accepting it had, however, to be taken seriously. Our range of products was wide. To feature every item prominently in every *Yellow Pages* directory throughout the country would make serious inroads into our total budget. To cater for one branch alone involved an expense that was far from negligible. It would be perfectly acceptable if it produced a commensurate result, and quite unacceptable if it did not. This seemed to be a situation that only an experiment could resolve.

I agreed that the branch could have the advertisements requested, but stipulated that the telephone number appearing in them should be not the normal number, but a separate line. This should cause no confusion because, by definition, the enquirers were unlikely to have heard of us beforehand, and once they were in correspondence the normal number would appear on all letterheads. To make the distinction perfectly clear internally we put a yellow telephone on the end of the special line, and instructed all staff to log every call received on that instrument.

After a few months, when only two calls had been recorded, it was accepted that at that particular time and for the specific products involved, anything more than a simple one-line entry in *Yellow Pages* was not justified. A similar measurement technique was however used later to prove the effectiveness of a major advertising campaign launching a new product. It was of course simply a development of the use of coded addresses or coupons, to identify the source of enquiries.

Measuring the number of enquiries or checking awareness ratings will enable judgements to be made of the relative success of different forms of advertising. What it will not do is tell you whether the expense as a whole was justified. The only measurement of that is the amount of business that can be attributed to advertising and would not have been forthcoming without it. We will undoubtedly look at the level of business before and after an advertising campaign, to see what increase if any has occurred. But this can be influenced by extraneous factors such as large orders which could have been maturing before the campaign even started, movements in the market as a whole, economic expectations or government legislation.

While large consumer companies can run campaigns in some areas but not in others to enable any increase due to advertising alone to be identified, most industrial firms cannot make controlled experiments of this kind. Their advertising tends to be national, in trade journals for example. By itself therefore, an increase in business will not prove that advertising works, or give a reliable indication of the value of orders that can be attributed to it. Likewise a decrease will not show that advertising has failed. Without it the position might have been much worse.

The link between advertisement and order What is needed is a chain linking advertisement to order. In some cases this can be established beyond a doubt and without a break. If specific enquiries are linked to a particular advertisement and then to a firm order, there is no difficulty, provided that an element of rough justice in the application of cut-off dates is accepted. When the responses to an advertisement are requests for information only in the first instance, and a firm enquiry may not follow for some months, it can be much harder to make a causal connection. Even if individual names could be traced through the whole process, other promotions may have taken place in the meantime and the customer may have forgotten how he or she first came to hear of the product. There could however be a statistical 'chain' which would yield meaningful information.

The lower links in such a chain are already in place. An order has been taken and will have stemmed from a firm enquiry and possibly from the despatch of a written quotation. So the numbers of firm enquiries or quotations can be recorded and compared with the number of orders taken. In this way the sales value of each quotation or enquiry is easily calculated. What then has to be established is a link between the appearance of an advertisement or the receipt of requests for information and firm enquiries or quotations.

If firm enquiries increase in number following an advertisement or bear a relationship to the number of requests for information, a statistical link can be made and ratios applied that will put a sales value on to every request for information that is received. This can then be compared with the cost of the advertisement.

As an example, suppose an advertisement costs £1000 and draws 200 requests for information. Whenever these are received it is noticed that in the third month following, firm enquiries increase by 10 per cent. Without this there are 80 firm enquiries a month, which produce £150 000 worth of sales from 16 orders. An extra 10 per cent represents 1.6 orders worth £15 000. So each of the 200 requests for information is worth £75 of business, and the cost of the advertisement (£1000) can be compared with the profit obtained from a sales value of £15 000.

Of course it will not be quite as neat as this, because the extent of the uplift in firm enquiries may have to be extracted after allowance has been made for seasonal or other factors, and it is doubtful whether the time-lag can be pinned down so accurately. The uplift may be spread over more than one month. Individual advertisements and the response they bring may also overlap for good, tactical reasons, which makes it difficult to isolate results. But in every organization there are figures available that can be studied and conclusions can be drawn that will shed light on the effectiveness of advertising expenditure.

What precisely these will be for any given company cannot be prescribed here. Some suggestions have been made, but a marketing manager who has mastered his or her craft will always be looking at figures to see when significant comparisons can be made. A steadfast intention to measure results will almost certainly produce more than one way of assessing the value of any advertising initiative. Not all methods will lead to firm conclusions of themselves, but taken together they will support a judgement which is far more informed than gut-feeling or plain prejudice.

A firm brief

Whether or not an agency is used any advertising should be preceded by a clear statement of objectives and an indication of how results will be assessed. These will of course be based on a great deal of background information and possibly on market research previously carried out. If an agency is employed as much as possible of this background will need to be made known, so that the agency has every opportunity to create something which is relevant. The brief might include:

- the target audience
- the product and its main benefits
- the company's current market share
- awareness of the company in the market place
- the company's reputation (if market research has been conducted)
- the company's main competitors
- competitors' products and sales approach
- competitors' reputation (again, if researched)
- main objective of the campaign
- how its success will be assessed
- budget available
- related promotions planned (e.g. exhibition, direct mail shot)
- specific need to integrate with other marketing activity (e.g. sales representative's approach, sales literature, demonstration techniques)

Tying in the loose ends

The main aims of integration will be achieved by working to well-considered objectives and measuring results. If all sales promotion is tackled systematically in this way, then the right amount of effort will be placed on every aspect, and everything should be geared to the company's broad marketing plan. Nevertheless when thinking of the brief to be given to advertisers it is necessary to be aware of what may be happening elsewhere inside, and outside, the marketing department. Even with a good, firm brief and an overall objective completely consistent with the aspirations of other members of the marketing team, things can go wrong unless steps are taken to foresee and prevent this.

In the first place, our pearls must be real, and seen as real by other members of the company. I recall a well-designed advertisement prepared by a leading American agency in my typewriter marketing days. It had been intended for use world-wide and was based on a briefing given in the USA. The caption read: 'Opens up like a book for easy and low-cost maintenance'. There was some truth in this, because our maintenance men were able to open up the machine, but the problem was they found it very difficult to put it back together again. Certainly no sales representative would have dared to demonstrate this salient feature. If you cannot believe your own slogan, what right have you to expect others to do so? Had we used the particular advertisement, the sales force would have been demoralized rather than encouraged.

In industrial selling the coordination of advertising with the efforts of the sales force is vital. Sales people need to see advertisements in line with the verbal claims they are making for the product. If a different approach has been suggested, and seems likely to produce better results, the whole sales team needs to be retrained before it is used. Where there is no such problem, we will still have to let sales people know exactly what is planned and how any enquiries that result are to be handled. If, for example, telephone enquiries are expected, staff need to be briefed on how to respond to them and how to record them.

Direct mail

Direct mail is the most easily integrated of all promotional methods. This is because it is flexible and can be despatched at any required rate to any given set of addresses. It also offers an advantage in measurability, since the target audience is precisely defined and responses are simple to trace. This makes it particularly useful in industrial selling where the market can often be delineated with great accuracy. The disadvantage is the cost of it.

Mailing can be used in a variety of ways to fulfil a number of objectives. With a simple enough product it can be used to obtain orders by return of post. More usually in industry, it can distribute information about a company's products, trawl for firm enquiries or pave the way for a direct sales approach. It can be despatched by an agency, from head or branch offices or by individual sales people. This extreme degree of flexibility does of course mean that the aims of any given campaign need to be clearly defined and that very close coordination with the sales force is usually required.

The exact objectives chosen depend on the size of the market and the degree to which potential customers are identifiable. There is a choice between:

1 Creating awareness of a company and of its stance in the market.

2 Distributing information on the company's products.

3 Producing enquiries for follow up by letter, telephone or personal call.

4 Preparing the way for a sales call.

5 Obtaining orders by post or telephone.

Although it might seem an expensive method of addressing the first two of these objectives, where prospects are limited in number and clearly defined there may be an argument for ensuring that each of them has a catalogue of the company's products to hand. Updating the catalogue with further mailing shots will reinforce the company's image and provide a further selling opportunity.

Granted that only a few industrial products will lend themselves to sales by post alone, as the last objective implies, it would seem that objectives 3 and 4 offer the greatest scope. Both need to be coordinated with sales people, but in the latter instance they can be completely under the control of individual salesmen or saleswomen. Where selling by direct approach is necessary, it is possible for representatives to plan their territory coverage so that letters are sent out in advance and followed in every case by telephone or personal calls. Direct mail then becomes simply another sales aid. But in a market of any size it would be arguably more efficient to give it a wider distribution and spend sales time only on those prospects who show initial interest.

However mailing is employed systems of measurement need to be installed to check results. The very nature of the technique makes measurement easier than with most other forms of promotion, but as always it is necessary for some one person to see that it happens. While sales people can be encouraged to recognize that any given order may have its origin in a mailing shot, the assessment of success or failure cannot be left to memory alone. So someone has to compare lists of names and addresses and ask questions where there is any doubt.

Sales literature

Sales leaflets have a large part to play in the exchange of information between seller and buyer. They can also be an essential aid to people engaged in face-to-face selling. Yet the way they are brought into being does not always exploit these potential advantages. The problem starts with design. Small companies which have created their own literature may not appreciate how much this shows. However good a marketing manager may be he or she is unlikely to be a commercial artist and neither is the printer who is often asked to stand in for one. Once this is appreciated the next step is often to put the production of literature in the hands of an advertising agency, if the company employs one. Indeed the agency's services could be needed more for this than for press advertising itself, and will in these circumstances justify a fee for the design work involved.

The new piece of literature then begins its life as a sample layout indicating where photographs, diagrams and graphic design features could be placed to create a well-balanced and satisfying appearance. The space reserved for copy and captions is indicated in 'printer's Latin'. All the emphasis at this stage is on how the leaflet will look when it is finished and what photographs will be included. The company eventually approves the layout and the next crisis is postponed until someone announces that definitive copy is required.

The agency may have been commissioned to produce copy as well as design but the dilemma is that the agency's copywriter knows nothing of the product, while the engineer or product manager, who knows all about the product, may lack writing skills. So when the copywriter presents a draft that does not satisfy the company a game of ping-pong is initiated, which carries the text to and fro until someone, usually at senior level, agrees that it is good enough. Time is by then at a premium so some compromise has to be made.

That this process results in even moderately satisfactory literature is remarkable. Usually changes have to be made at subsequent reprints, which increase the long-term cost of the project. But it is not the cost nor the waste of managerial time that is the most disturbing feature. It is that the entire process is being tackled upside down. It may be only at the last moment that an attempt is made to see that the leaflet is in line with the marketing objectives of the company.

Faced with enthusiastic publicity officers, account executives and designers, all keen to start from the wrong end, a marketing manager might well consider the possibility of insisting on a written 'literature brief' for each new project. This would start with the market and move more logically towards the content of a proposed leaflet, without putting too many constraints on the designer. It could cover:

- the target audience: buyers, purchasing influencers, dealers, etc.
- uses to which the leaflet will be put
  –by the customer (kept for reference, used to specify or make decision)
  –by the company (sent through the post, used by representatives)
- the product or products it will display
- features and benefits to be covered
- key benefits to be highlighted
- other company leaflets, data sheets, etc. to which reference should be made
- competitive literature currently available.

This should ensure that design and copy are seen as a whole, and that the use of the leaflet as a marketing tool is fully understood.

As an illustration of the detailed way in which the literature brief can prove effective we might look at leaflets sent to architects. These are invariably kept for reference and the hope is that they will be used to specify the product when a need arises. So they should have the correct, standard classification to find the right place in the architect's files, but there are other requirements. If they are to be placed in ring binders, thought has to be given to the layout to ensure that the leaflet can still be clearly read and that vital parts of the sales message are not then obscured. Their descriptions and diagrams have to be clear and easy for a specifier to reproduce; in addition the benefits highlighted may have to appeal both to the architect and the client. All of which is far removed from simply choosing some nice looking photographs and producing a handsome layout.

Similarly, if a leaflet is to be used by a sales representative talking to potential customers, the order in which the information it contains is presented is important. If the customer's attention is drawn away from rather than towards the point the representative is making, you have created a sales handicap rather than a sales aid, no matter how good the leaflet may be in other respects.

The literature brief should see that points like these are not overlooked, whatever decisions are finally taken. If it is strong enough, it may be possible to use freelance designers or copywriters working under the eye of the marketing manager. This could be helpful to the small firm which might find it hard to interest an advertising agency when what is needed is primarily literature design. But in all circumstances it will ensure that the leaflet is an integrated piece of sales promotion.

PR

Some of its practitioners have been content to leave the term PR without a precise definition. It might mean public relations, and that indeed is the concern of the finest exponents of the art: the relations a company has with the public at large or with influential sections of it. Public relations experts lobby Parliament, put the mind of the City at rest, gain the acceptance of the local community and generally work to improve a company's image. Their services are expensive and tend to be purchased by large corporations or bodies with some very special pleading to do.

For most medium- or small-sized industrial companies PR means press relations or even press releases. What such companies want is editorial coverage of their products and services, which increases awareness of their existence and enhances their reputation. Unless a company has a writer among its employees who knows what it is that journals like to receive and publish, it would be wise to turn to a specialist PR agency for work of this kind. The difficulty is that some agencies act as if what they are offering is public relations in its widest and grandest sense, while what they deliver is something much more modest. Consequently they will want to deal with the managing director, especially if he or she is not averse to a little personal PR. Regular reports, in nicely padded covers, detailing their efforts will then be presented to the managing director. If such reports are examined critically they will often be seen to be concerned with input, not output. The impression created is of an ongoing activity, important to the company's well-being, but not subject to measurement, or at least to the cruder forms of measurement to which other parts of marketing are exposed.

Naturally if this stance is once allowed it will be difficult, if not impossible, for a marketing manager to integrate PR into the overall marketing operation. At best it is not easy to do so. There is the obvious problem of ensuring that what appears in the press is in line with product and marketing policy. Even insisting on approving every press release before it is sent out does not guarantee this because, as any PR expert will explain, you cannot control what is actually printed in journals. It will however entail a good deal of rewriting to remove errors of fact or over-enthusiastic claims for the product.

A greater impediment to integration is the genuine difficulty of measuring the results of PR. Here is an activity which costs money and has therefore to compete for its share of available resources, yet does not appear susceptible to any method of comparing its effectiveness with that of other promotional tools. Measurement of some kind is necessary if PR is to be taken seriously. In its absence decisions may be made on emotional grounds, for example through resentment of an error appearing in print, rather than on the basis of what PR can really contribute.

The solution, as with other forms of promotion, is to take firm charge. PR needs clear objectives just as much as press advertising or direct mail. In special circumstances these may extend beyond those relating the company to its potential or actual customers, and include legislators or the financial world.

Although in the case of PR the emphasis may be different, commonly they will be identical to those set for advertising, namely:

- to create awareness of the company and its products
- to reinforce a favourable image of the company
- to obtain enquiries.

Once objectives are accepted some of the measurements used elsewhere may be considered. PR can often produce identifiable enquiries, but even where it is not easy to separate enquiries stemming from PR from those originating from other sources, less direct methods can be applied. An examination of enquiries received before, during and after a PR campaign may provide a rough indication of success or failure. Market research can, as before, reveal changes in awareness or reputation ratings. Even if an improvement may be not solely due to PR, lack of improvement would certainly prove something.

A still cruder measure often applied is press 'mileage'. This at least reveals how much information is getting into print, and most PR agencies will be willing to provide evidence in the form of press cuttings. In itself this is an aid to integration since, as has been said in Chapter 4, cuttings can be distributed to all marketing people, and throughout the entire organization. Nevertheless mileage cannot be accepted as a measure of success without qualification. Not all column inches are equal. Mention of a company's products in a free trade journal or a local newspaper is hardly the equivalent of an article featuring the company in a leading national daily, or a minute or two of favourable comment on television.

That is of course a qualitative judgement, but it may be appropriate, when firmer measurements are not available, to look at qualitative ways of discerning the good from the mediocre. This will at least put some value on what is otherwise just a figure representing an area covered in black ink. One system that I found effective was to collect press cuttings and then, at regular intervals, to sit down with the PR specialist concerned and classify every item. For this a scale was needed to indicate the likely impact of the item itself and the importance of the journal in which it had appeared. We used the following scale.

A Favourable application story in a leading journal, e.g. *Financial Times*

B Good write-up in less influential publication

C+ Good product release in trade press

C− Routine product release, not so well featured

D Mention in *Little Twaddlestock Echo*

X Unfavourable news items, e.g. a strike at the factory

We had naturally to agree on the definitions and codes used, and to use them consistently. There is a subjective element in every judgement made, but if the exercise is repeated each time by the same two people, and if they obtain genuine agreement on each item, progress can be charted.

This routine is not going to produce a financial justification of the

PR budget, but it will enable the material appearing in print to be assessed against a set of objectives. If the aim is to increase the proportion of A and B items while maintaining the number of those rated C+, each meeting will be looking for evidence that this is happening. This single technique has in itself a stimulating effect on the PR agency. It is far removed from an uncritical acceptance of reports detailing PR effort, or of unclassified press mileage.

Such a method of checking progress against objectives, coupled with a hard look at enquiries received as a direct result of press releases, and periodic research into the company's image in the market-place, will do much to make PR an integrated part of marketing policy. It should then be easier to persuade the sales force to help find material for A and B type stories.

At the same time a clear eye needs to be kept on the actual releases sent out. If any are off-target and fail to represent the product correctly, the result may be a host of enquiries for something the sales department cannot supply. A small misunderstanding and a clumsy choice of words can cause a disproportionate amount of ill will among members of the sales force who have to explain that the press 'got it wrong'.

Although the ultimate sanction on whatever is released must lie with the marketing manager, the need to use it will be reduced by shorter lines of communication. As discussed in Chapter 4 it makes good sense for the PR specialist to deal directly with sales representatives and their customers where application stories are concerned. It will also be wise to involve the product manager in anything which is written about his or her products.

Exhibitions

A good exhibition follows a tradition extending back beyond the medieval fair, and carries echoes of the excitement and sense of occasion that has always attended such events. It might also be a manifestation of the human herd instinct, and as such should be treated by the marketor with a certain amount of caution. The fact that your competitors are all going to be there is not, in itself, sufficient reason for attending. This is all the more so when new exhibitions and new venues proliferate. Anyone can set up an exhibition, and usually those who do are expecting to make money from exhibitors. In the case of shows organized by bodies such as trade associations there may be an element of self-aggrandisement as well.

Yet when an exhibition is announced marketing managers often find themselves on the defensive, having to explain to the managing director and to their sales staff just why it is they are not keen to accept this or that opportunity to meet thousands of prospective customers. Logically the onus should be on making a case for entering rather than for staying out, but logic does not always prevail in this particular field: the herd instinct is too strong.

It is often assumed that if all your competitors are there, you *must* be there. If you are not, this will leave the field wide open to others and damage your credibility in the eyes of your customers. This is an especially strong reaction when the exhibition is a well-established one in which the company has participated for several years. No one then asks if you are going to take space this year, only how much space you will need.

There are of course often good reasons for participating, whether an exhibition is old established or brand new. But they need to be thought out afresh, every time. Otherwise an exhibition can become a most unintegrated part of the marketing programme, more likely to disrupt than to supplement the efforts being made elsewhere. This is all the more so because the true cost of an exhibition is hard to calculate. The charge for the stand space, the cost of designing and erecting the stand, travel and subsistence expenses are all easy enough to identify. But exhibitions are time-consuming. The stand is manned by sales people and managers who would normally be elsewhere, doing other things to obtain business. Managers are also involved in planning meetings and briefings, under the pressure generated by a fixed deadline. When all this time and energy is taken into account, as well as the known costs, the calculation becomes complex. It is not enough to estimate a proportion of the wages and overheads of those participating. The value of the work they would otherwise have done also needs consideration. To justify this sacrifice, an exhibition needs objectives that are just as clear as for any other form of promotion, and its results have to be assessed with care.

There are valid reasons for attending, based once again on the information requirements of potential customers. If in order to make buying decisions it is necessary to see a product and to compare it with others, an exhibition may be one of the most convenient ways of achieving this. A person interested in buying a boat may visit the Boat Show to look at a number of suitable craft. To call on the manufacturers of half a dozen boats would take days of travel: here they are all within short walking distance of each other. From the other side, boatbuilders who would otherwise find it hard to identify prospects are assured that among the thousands visiting the show there will be a number of serious buyers. For the boatbuilder the objective is quite clear and the measurement of success will lie in the number of boats sold either at the show, or as a direct result of the show.

In industrial selling there may be no such clarity. It may not be possible to take orders on the stand itself, because although the product may be displayed, fitting it to any given customer's requirements might take much longer and involve surveys or investigations on site. In some instances all that can be hoped for is firm enquiries, coupled with a greater awareness of the company and its products and possibly an improved impression of its capabilities. And, as we have seen, there are other ways of achieving objectives like these. So if an exhibition is not going to yield orders, either now or in the near future, its full cost ought to be weighed against the cost of other means of promoting sales.

Similar considerations apply to local or to private exhibitions. If they perform a useful service to buyer and seller alike, these smaller and cheaper exercises may be worth while, but that has to be proved by results. As we have seen they may require a special effort from the sales force to ensure that potential customers are invited and do in fact attend. The cost of time spent on this has also to be taken into account.

An exhibition, national or local, public or private, constitutes a good test of the mechanics of integration. It needs sales people to man it, and often additional publicity and PR to maximize its chances of success. If new products are to be shown, the entire procedure for launching them has to be geared to a fixed date, which puts a strain on Engineering and Production as well as on Marketing. The effort to produce a finished example of the product, complete with sales literature and price information in time for the opening of a major exhibition has proved too much for many an otherwise efficient organization.

Sales aids

Sales aids can range from sight-sellers carrying text, diagrams or photographs, through video presentations to samples of the product, demonstration kits, or complete working models. Mainly they are tools for the sales people to use in the field, but sometimes they may have to work on their own, as when, for example, a sample is left with a customer or a machine is installed on a trial basis.

Their production can easily fall into a vacuum between departments, with Manufacturing unwilling to direct effort to making samples, for instance, while Sales need them urgently to obtain orders. Their cost may not always be formally included in the publicity budget, and for that reason sometimes escapes the scrutiny it merits. Yet even humble tools of the trade, like sight-sellers, can be expensive to produce when they are wanted in comparatively small quantities. Once more the justification for such expense lies in the information customers need before they can make a buying decision. Will the product be better understood, and valued more highly, as a result of using a sales aid? If the answer is affirmative we might then go on to ask: 'And will the sales aid be used in practice?' Too many of these tools start life as a bright idea on the part of someone in head office and end life languishing in the boot of a representative's car.

There is no point in producing a demonstration kit that is so tricky to use that a salesman fears it may lose him the sale. All such kits need to be tested in the field with full consideration given to the views of sales people. Training in their use has to be provided, and checks made to see how they are being incorporated into the selling sequence. One of the advantages of the field visits advocated in Chapter 4 is that they enable the use of sales aids to be observed in live selling situations. It is of course highly desirable that the marketing manager should be adept in using any aid the sales force is expected to carry.

Mix and match

Marketing has at its disposal a formidable range of promotional tools:

- the sales force itself
- sales literature
- other sales aids
- exhibitions
- direct mail
- advertising
- PR.

Each can be considered as an alternative to one or more of the others. A choice has to be made and those that are chosen have to be blended into a coherent marketing approach.

To make the choice from scratch would require an examination of the size and nature of the market, how many potential buyers exist, how easily they can be identified and what information needs they have. Fortunately most companies have access to past experience and this can be used, along with a realistic estimate of comparative costs. It does however depend on its being factual, recorded experience and not a sales myth. In all cases there is scope for experiment, provided that the mechanism for some form of measurement is in place. As resources are always limited there is no room for sacred cows. Any that do not produce milk should be slaughtered without delay.

After deciding the basic mix it is necessary to ensure that the various elements in it work smoothly together. The use made of sales promotion by the sales force is often the key to this. Sales people use sales literature and sales aids directly, work at exhibitions and follow up direct mail or advertising enquiries. Their attitudes, and the training given to them, will do much to determine the success or failure of promotional exercises.

In deploying resources across a range of marketing activity it is necessary to see that the simplest of all measures to ensure integration is not ignored. This is that the same message is carried by all media, and that this same message will be used by sales people when facing customers. If the objectives set for everything from advertising to sales aids have defined clearly the market and the company's approach to it, common goals should have been established. Then when an enquiry is received, it will be for something a sales representative can sell, and will come from a prospect who has a good idea of what to expect when the representative calls.

What external help do you need?

A determination to take full charge of the promotional budget and decide precisely what the mix will be is one thing. The skill needed to design advertisements or sales literature or to write good copy is another. Sometimes a simple advertisement can be produced in-house, perhaps using a portion of an existing sales leaflet as an attention-getter, but sales literature itself has a more permanent function and needs good design. If there is not much advertising to be done you could therefore seek the services of a freelance literature designer rather than an advertising agency, or a you might find an agency willing to tailor its work to your needs, for a fair reward.

PR needs a specialist, but a freelance PR expert could also double as a copywriter. It is possible for a very small company to choose freely from the full range of promotional techniques without involving an advertising agency at all. It depends on what you want to achieve, and on the contacts you can make with people who will help and who are known to be reliable.

If you have to look for a suitable agency to handle advertising, there is something to be said for letting the chosen agency deal with your other promotional needs, provided that it is able and willing to do so. Familiarity with the company should prove a plus point, and fewer briefings will be required. The dangers inherent in this course are greatly lessened when the marketing manager is firmly in control and both objectives and means of measurement have been established separately for all activities. The agency then has the assurance that everything it does will be taken seriously and also the chance to request exemption from any area in which it feels less than completely competent.

In selecting an agency it is desirable to ensure that your account is large enough to be of continuing interest, but not so large that the existence of the agency is entirely dependent upon your work. However attractive that might seem, in the long run over-anxiety tends to stifle initiative and gets in the way of a clear view of what the market needs. An inspection of the agency will tell you whether the services offered are all produced in-house or subcontracted. If they are subcontracted, it does not mean that inferior people are employed, but it might prompt you to think of getting some services directly rather than through the agency.

However services are purchased, the more open the discussion can be and the more information that can be given about the company and its plans the better. Integrating outside specialists into the marketing programme has many similarities with what needs to be done internally to make things work.

Questions and action points for decision takers

Advertising discipline

Is your market small and compact or widespread?

Are prospects hard to locate?

Have you considered whether you really need press advertising?

What is the prime objective of your advertising:

- to create awareness of your company and its products
- to reinforce a favourable image
- to obtain enquiries?

How will results be measured:

- by number of enquiries obtained
- through research to check awareness ratings or reputation
- in some other way?

Have you considered a wider use of:

- special telephone numbers
- coded or couponed advertisements?

What procedures exist to make sure all enquiries are recorded?

Can you identify the value of business resulting from advertising?

Does the brief given to the agency include:

- the target audience
- the product and its main benefits
- the company's current market share
- awareness of the company in the market place
- the company's reputation (if researched)
- main objective of the campaign
- how its success will be measured
- budget available
- related promotion

- specific integration needs
- other factors of importance to you?

Are advertisements in line with the current sales approach?

If there are changes, has the sales force been retrained?

Have sales staff been fully briefed on the campaign?

Direct mail

Can direct mail be used to:

- create awareness
- distribute information
- produce enquiries
- pave the way for sales calls
- obtain immediate orders?

What is the main objective of your campaign?

How will the results be measured?

Who is in charge of this?

Sales literature

How is the new sales literature initiated?

Is there a literature brief covering:

- target audience
- how the leaflet will be used
  –by the customer
  –by the company
- product(s) to be displayed
- features and benefits
- key benefits
- other company literature to which reference is needed
- competitive literature
- other factors of importance?

PR

What objectives have been set for PR?

What can be done to measure success?

Can enquiries generated by PR be identified?

Are press cuttings

- collected
- distributed to the sales force, and others?

Are press cuttings classified to establish their relative value?

Who does this?

Are all press releases checked at senior level before despatch?

Exhibitions

What exhibitions are currently attended?

How much sales/management time is involved?

What objectives are set?

How are results measured?

Have alternative methods of promotion been considered?

Sales aids

How are sales aids related to the information needs of customers?

Are sales people trained in their use?

Are they actually being used?

Can their full cost be identified?

Are the results of all alternative methods of promotion recorded?

Mix and Match

Is the information sufficient to enable decisions to be made?

What further experiments are necessary?

Does all promotion carry a common message?

Using an agency

Do you need an advertising agency?

Could sales literature, PR etc, be handled by freelance specialists?

Should the agency be responsible for all promotion?

How important to the agency is your account?

How open are you in dealing with the agency or other outside specialists?

6

Facts and the confusion they cause

The role of market research

Market research is a quest for knowledge. It may be knowledge of what is happening in markets where a company is already established, or of new markets it is thinking of joining; but in every case the assumption is that decisions will be better made with knowledge than without. So why is it that for much of industry market research is at best a one-off event, producing a report to be filed away, rather than an integral part of everyday business life?

A number of reasons will be given whenever this question is put. Research costs money and takes time. Either might be in short supply when any given decision has to be made. Research can involve the use of outside specialists, and the person commissioning it may have little experience in choosing people for this kind of work. In this way another layer of uncertainty is added in evaluating the results obtained. Those results may in themselves be indeterminate; the key decision to be made can remain a matter of judgement even when all the facts surrounding it are known.

Any of these objections could in certain circumstances be valid and they will be addressed later in this chapter. Yet it seems unlikely that they are collectively sufficient to explain the poor use made of market research in industry. Often they are little more than a smoke-screen to hide a deeper aversion to the search for truth.

Barriers to research

A fear of knowledge

Not everyone in business has been trained to value objectivity. In an ethos where strength of will is seen to have a greater survival value than intellect, winning the argument can take precedence over checking the facts.

Let us make a distinction between two types of business behaviour, defensive and aggressive. Of course such a crude dichotomy is over-simplistic where people are concerned, but it can be applied to the situations in which they find themselves, and may help to explain attitudes to market research.

Regardless of personality, a marketing manager who has been at the helm for a number of years has something to defend. It will be assumed that he or she knows a great deal about the market and the company's place in it. Statements will have been made and figures quoted. Others will tend to look to the marketing manager for guidance and to assume a depth of knowledge which is seldom put to the test, at least while sales remain high. It takes a certain freshness of mind, if not courage, to admit ignorance and initiate a research programme which could undermine a stance which has previously been accepted without question.

There are times when the entrenched infallibility of senior management can lead to absurdity. Once, as a young man, I joined an organization in the fond hope of introducing marketing into the system. On my first day I asked what research had been done to measure the size of the market as a whole. 'Oh, if you want to know that,' came the reply, 'you should go and talk to Mr X.' Mr X was the sales director, a man of standing in the industry and as kindly a character as any young marketor could have wished to consult. 'You want to know the size of the market?' he asked with gentle surprise. 'Well it's £5 000 000 a year.' With some temerity I inquired: 'How do we know that?' 'Oh,' he said, 'It's simple. Our sales last year were £2 500 000 and we always get 50 per cent.' It was clearly the end of the interview.

This may be an extreme case. There was no chance whatsoever of instituting any research into that company's performance in the market-place. It does however indicate the problems that can stem from *ex officio* defensiveness. The most magisterial pronouncements of senior marketing figures can be based on little more than wishful thinking.

Unfortunately pressure from more 'aggressive' managers rarely serves as a corrective. Happy as they may be to deride their more defensive colleagues, they are equally unlikely to welcome research, except on occasions when it might be used to discomfort an opponent.

Entrepreneurial attitudes

The chief of the large group I subsequently served would undoubtedly have classed himself as aggressive and as a decision-maker. Whether he would really have been happy if all his subordinates had been cast in a similar mould is open to question, but he certainly had no time for hesitation. Not without reason he viewed the employment of consultants as a way of postponing decisions that had to be made. The virtual ban on consultancy extended to market research agencies: 'a managing director ought to know his markets without outside help.' Nothing of course was said about markets in which the company did not yet participate, or how knowledge of them was to be acquired.

Here I have to make a short but relevant digression. A ban on the use of research agencies was in the event one of the best things that could have happened to me. I had to learn how to conduct simple market studies myself, and to make sure that none of the expense involved appeared in the accounts under the heading of consultancy. As a result I came to see how much useful work can be done inexpensively in-house, and to appreciate better when and where outside help is really needed. These are matters which will be discussed in more detail later.

All business decisions are made with imperfect information. It is one thing to accept this as a fact, another altogether to elevate it to the status of a virtue. But the image of the strong, entrepreneurial manager sizing up a situation and coming to a crisp decision has its obvious attractions. Business games have tended to reinforce what is in reality a very old-fashioned concept. They seldom reward the player who says: 'No one but a fool would make a decision on the basis of the information you have provided. I am therefore going to do nothing until I have conducted some research to remedy this deficiency.'

So on the one hand we have people who are supposed to know the essential facts about their markets and on the other people who are trained to see merit in instant decision making. Against this unpromising background the market research industry has not always presented its case well. It has been more concerned with what it has to offer and less with what customers might welcome if given the chance. Formal surveys of a highly standardized kind, conducted entirely outside the client company, have been the norm until quite recently. They have been expensive and sometimes ineffective in terms of the action that has followed them. That may not have been the fault of the researchers, but it has contributed to making market research the most unintegrated marketing activity of all.

Grasping the nettle

The way out of this quandary has already been charted in dealing with other aspects of integration. The marketing manager has to take the lead in defining in detail what market research is required and how it will be done. This does not imply taking the path which, under pressure, I followed, and making research a hobby. Interesting as it is, you may have other subjects which demand time and attention. Few marketing managers can become equally expert at all aspects of their crafts. A firm working knowledge of what is needed and a resolve to see it happen by one means or another will in most circumstances suffice.

To grasp this particular nettle we have to consider:

1 What information research can provide, i.e. its broad scope.

2 The uses to which this information can be put.

3 The methods by which answers can be found to the questions posed.

Subsequently it should become easier to see if and when agencies should be employed, and how the best value can be obtained from them.

The scope of market research

We have already touched upon some aspects of market research in earlier chapters. The information it can provide is both quantitative and qualitative. *Quantitative* research was examined in Chapter 3 where we were considering one of its main uses, as a basis for sound sales forecasting. Its scope was illustrated diagrammatically in Figure 3.1. Here a wider field of application in strategic planning will need to be taken into account. At this stage however the content of a quantitative market analysis will be listed again as a reminder. It includes:

- potential: ultimate and immediate
- penetration to date
- annual sales in total
- new and replacement components of annual sales
- trends in total sales
- competitors' shares of total sales
- trends in competitors' shares.

Armed with this information a picture can be constructed of the market as a whole and of the position of other participants in it. It is however a purely quantitative picture at this stage. The dynamics which have created it and which will shape its future have yet to be considered.

Qualitative market analysis

It is possible to examine both our customers and our competitors more closely. As will be seen this can be one of the easier tasks of market research, but the yield it produces can be of vital importance, both strategically and tactically. It will also be necessary to look at various influencing factors which may impinge on the market in future.

Competitors' selling methods and pricing practices How products are sold at present and at what prices are important questions. Of course it is not obligatory to follow existing selling methods or to sell at current market prices, but it would be unwise to ignore what others are doing. What should be researched is not, as we shall see, simply how competitors sell, but how they could sell if they came under more severe attack.

Similarly with pricing, the question to be asked is not what prices are shown in a published price list, but what is actually charged. And it would be desirable to go further if possible and estimate the profit margins obtained by competitors, to form a view of the prices that might in future be charged, if the going became hard. Many of these aspects may be quite well understood for markets in which a company has experience, but they need research if new markets are contemplated.

Customer buying motives What do customers really want from a product? Your sales people will tell you, but as has been mentioned in Chapter 4, they may not tell you the truth, or they may themselves have been misled. At the very least they will have been unduly influenced by customers they have recently seen, who may have been far from representative of the market as a whole.

It is all too easy to come to the conclusion that what a customer wants is a product with all the features and benefits of every competitive offering, but at a lower price than is currently charged by anyone. To cope with practicalities your information needs to be more discerning. It would be worth knowing how customers rate these various features and benefits against each other, what they like or dislike about competitors' products, service or selling methods, and how loyal they are to choices previously made.

Customer buying practices An investigation of potential will have indicated the customers who are likely to buy a product, either now or in the future. But within the customer's organization who makes the buying decision? And how much information is needed before a decision can be made? Further questions might ask how the information required is normally obtained, how suppliers are contacted and how orders are placed. Answers to queries of this kind have implications for all aspects of marketing.

Awareness and reputation The attitude of customers to competitors in the field has already been mentioned. Research can take enquiries further in this direction to include factors likely to be of importance in planning promotional campaigns and in identifying the company's own strengths and weaknesses.

How aware are customers of our company and of its competitors? The first step in a marketing plan may have to be convincing potential buyers of the very existence of the company as a credible supplier. Reputation can also be examined, assuming the necessary awareness is there. The company and its competitors can be rated against a list of factors relevant to the customers they serve: reliability, for example, or running costs or technical assistance. And customers can be asked to rate these factors in order of importance. The net result is not simply a tool to improve the effectiveness of sales promotion; it is something which can furnish all departments in the company with a common goal, directed towards customer satisfaction.

Product trends Research into product trends may, as we have seen in Chapter 1, take place as much in the laboratory as in the market. Market research into products which do not yet exist is fraught with problems. But once an idea becomes tangible it is possible to test the receptiveness of customers to it. This may not be the easiest area for industrial research, yet it can be vital. In an age of rapid technological advance, bright ideas proliferate: some of them however, are not good ideas. If those without a future can be eliminated, effort can be concentrated where it will stand the best chance of producing something people will really want.

Market threats and opportunities A market can be affected by events and trends impinging on it from outside, just as much as by technical development within. To detect threats and opportunities of this kind we have to look further than our existing customers, although their comments may shed some light on what may lie ahead.

Government rules and regulations may have significance. We looked at the effect of some of these when discussing sales forecasting in Chapter 3. Often they create threats and opportunities at one and the same time. The requirement to fit rear seat belts in motor cars will have enlarged the market for suppliers of seat belts. It will not, however, have enlarged the market for cars. Instead it will have increased overall prices and affected the differential in price between small and larger cars.

Technical development outside the market altogether may yet have consequences for it. The existence of higher quality telephone lines switched through electronic exchanges has provided opportunities for a new range of services from banks, security companies or providers of information and entertainment. To anticipate developments like these demands a broad view of what is happening in the world and occasional help from technical experts. It may not be textbook market research, but it is still a research task.

In summary, the scope of market research is to find information on a number of quantitative and qualitative issues that can affect a company's marketing strategy:

Quantitative

- Potential: ultimate and immediate
- Penetration to date
- Annual sales

- New and replacement components of sales
- Trends in total sales
- Competitors' shares of sales
- Trends in competitors' shares

Qualitative

- Competitors' selling methods
- Competitors' pricing policies
- Customer buying motives
- Customer buying practices
- Awareness and reputation
- Product trends
- Market threats and opportunities

Armed with this information marketing planning becomes, if not a science, at least something far removed from the expression of whim or prejudice. Defensive or aggressive attitudes are not eliminated, but, against a background of knowledge, the stance adopted can be seen for what it is, and evaluated accordingly.

The uses of research

The research yield has significance for others beside marketing planners. Because of this it can become a binding agent in the integration of marketing throughout the company. Let us examine the practical use to which market research can be put:

- in overall planning
- by departments outside Marketing
- by the marketing department itself.

Then, once the effort has been seen to be worthwhile, we can go on to look at ways of answering the research questions that have been posed.

Strategic planning

One of the principal methods of strategic planning is to forecast results if no policy changes are made, then identify any gaps that may leave between the profit anticipated and the aspirations of those in charge of the company. Forecasting was discussed in Chapter 3 along with the contribution quantitative market research can make towards it. In strategic planning it is desirable to take this process a stage further, and consider the life cycle of each product in the range. Every product goes through stages of growth, maturity and decay. A knowledge of where each is in its cycle can do more than improve overall forecasts. It can predict when and where specific gaps are going to occur.

A typical instance is shown in Figure 6.1. Here it has been assumed that the product has been an immediate success. It might easily have taken longer to become established than the graph indicates. Eventually there must come a time when growth slows. Here, after a peak in the third year, sales decline, first slowly and then more rapidly as alternatives become increasingly attractive to customers.

It will be noted that sales are the same at points A and C, yet the situation is very different. It should not be difficult to recognize whether you are on the ascent or the decline at these points. Just how far you have to go upwards and how fast you will be coming down may be more difficult to predict. One of the key points at which correct judgement is needed is B. Looking purely at annual sales, all that may be seen here is a blip, a temporary reduction in the rate of increase. Given knowledge of available potential and penetration to this point it might be possible to diagnose the first

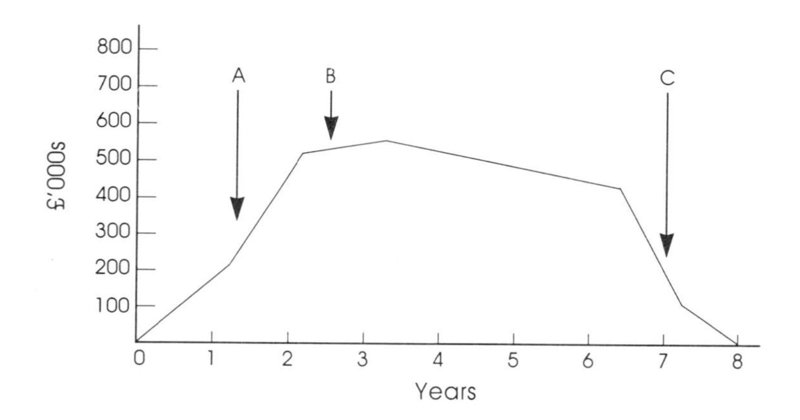

Figure 6.1 Product life cycle

signs of 'top-out'. Intelligence on competitors' sales and production capacity, and on any indications of price cutting, would help to confirm the position. Then action can be taken, for if a product is in decline, new products or new markets are needed to ensure continued growth.

Strategic planning is not a matter of figures alone. Qualitative market research is also needed if correct decisions are to be made. This is especially the case when entering new markets. Naturally research will look at competitors' selling methods and pricing policies, but this has to be more than a superficial glance. As discussed earlier, we need to be able to anticipate how competitors are likely to behave when faced with our own attack on their home territory. Failure to do so can lead to disaster.

In my early days selling office equipment, the firm for which I worked decided to diversify by adding office duplicating machines to its range. The market was then shared by two major competitors who sold both duplicators and the supplies needed to operate them, stencils, inks and paper. We obtained the distributorship of a Danish machine which offered some technical advantages, especially for colour work. A team of enthusiastic salesmen was recruited and trained in demonstrating the advantages of the new machine. It was offered at a price comparable to that of its competitors, which left an adequate margin for the company. Initial reaction from potential customers was very good indeed. The product, when installed, worked perfectly. So why did we have to close the division down within six months of the product launch?

It was no fault of the product, or its manufacturer or of the salesmen concerned. Instead it was a fault of market intelligence, a lack of understanding of the business our competitors were in. We believed they were in the duplicator business, when in fact they were in the paper business. For years the bulk of their profit had come from the supplies they sold. All service and equipment guarantees were geared to the use of their branded papers and inks. This was known, of course, and we had looked forward to the growth of supplies business as a useful extra. Its much greater financial significance to our competitors had not been appreciated.

We were a threat to a highly profitable business in paper, but only if we sold machines. Since the market had already attained a high degree of penetration, most machine business was replacement business. In bidding for it against the incumbent participants we became a highly visible target for price-cutting. Our competitors were prepared if necessary to give machines away to protect their supplies business and deny us a foothold in the market. We had either to accept losses for an indefinite period until we could build up a sufficient machine base ourselves, or to withdraw. As we were not in the paper business we pulled out.

Strategic planning is therefore able to benefit from both quantitative and qualitative research. This becomes of vital importance when new products are contemplated, but it is hard to see value in any projections made without some insight into the market that goes a good deal further than extrapolating past sales figures and joining the dots.

Design and development

Research can do more than help to indicate a general need for new products. Although it has been argued that it is not often itself a source of new product ideas, it can assist in defining the potential for projects that may have their origins in Engineering or elsewhere. And it can certainly discover what customers want from existing products and where improvements might be made with profit.

In the later stages of development the methods of market research can be employed in market acceptance tests, to ensure that the product, as designed, is likely to find a place in the market when it is launched.

Production

Soundly based forecasts are of obvious interest to manufacturing managers. In as far as market research may have contributed to them its relevance is easily demonstrated. It has earlier been suggested that openness on the part of product managers and others in explaining the basis on which their forecasts have been constructed can only lead to greater confidence in the factory, and to improved relationships between Marketing and Production.

A more immediate impact may be made by research into customers' views of the products they receive. Elaborate quality systems will avail little if the quality they guarantee is not what the customer wants. Research can look at this, on its own or as part of a package which includes features, or ease of operation. The evidence provided can influence manufacturing priorities in a way that no harangue from a marketing manager is ever likely to do. It is one way of bringing the customer closer to the factory.

Installation and service

The importance attached by customers to installation or after-sales service as aspects of a complete sales package can be checked. As with quality, the standards expected from suppliers can be clarified and the company's performance rated against that of its competitors.

Financial planning

The relevance of research to sales and thus to financial forecasts has been stressed sufficiently already. There are however other aspects of financial planning which benefit from market information. How orders are placed and on what terms may be common knowledge in existing markets but when a new venture is being considered these aspects need investigation. If, for example, orders are in the form of standard contracts which, as in the building industry, allow for the retention of a percentage of the money owed for a period of some months after completion, this has to be allowed for in predicting cash flow.

The sales force

Whether a sales force is needed or not depends on the information requirements of potential customers. It may also be influenced by the current practices of competitors. Both aspects can be researched and should be, from time to time. What sort of a sales force is needed is related to the way in which buying decisions are made. The person to whom the sale has to be made will determine the type of representative needed and the extent of any training which has to be given.

Sales representatives are often given targets. If these are seen to be based on a realistic appreciation of the market and to be achievable, they will act as an incentive. Sharing research information with the sales team thus helps to motivate its members in their task.

Research can also be used to correct the misapprehensions that occur from time to time. When sales fall away, everything tends to seem for the worst in the worst of all possible markets. It is easy then to believe that the market is saturated, that the company's prices are too high, or that one or two competitors are virtually invincible. Research, conducted objectively and fully discussed, can set the record straight. Naturally if any of the worries sales people have are *not* misapprehensions, action which goes farther than reassurance will need to be taken.

The greatest benefit so far as the sales force is concerned may come from qualitative research. In addition to identifying decision makers it can help to build the sales story. Quite simple research can pinpoint what it is about a product that customers like, or do not like, and how they see the company and its competitors. Properly and positively handled this information can be used to construct a stronger sales presentation.

Sales promotion

The same information is of course highly relevant to any advertising or PR campaign that is being planned. But research can do more still for sales promotion. By identifying the media of interest to potential customers it can save a great deal of money which might otherwise be spent in experimentation. It can also supply some of the measurement which is necessary to judge the effectiveness of campaigns. Where the objective has been to lift awareness or enhance the company's reputation, broad progress can be assessed by follow-up research.

There is much in common between the needs of different departments, from Production right through to Advertising. Reliable findings about the size of the market or the likely reaction of customers to improvements in the product itself, the service which accompanies it, or the information supplied to prospective users, relate to almost everything a company does. Indeed there has to be a common theme if the company is to make the right product and tell customers about it in a clear and unified way. Market research then becomes a prime factor in achieving integrated marketing.

We should in consequence look at ways of doing it which avoid, or at least limit the effect of, the real objections set out at the beginning of this chapter. It is proposed to do this by taking in turn each of the items listed earlier as falling within the scope of research, and seeing how in each case answers can be found to the questions raised. Then it may be appropriate to examine more generally what can be achieved in-house and where it may be advisable to use research agencies.

Finding the answers

Potential

Before potential can be estimated it has to be defined specifically for every product. We have to decide who the users are likely to be and how they will use the product. This is a matter of judgement and cannot be left entirely to an outside agency. Indeed most research agencies are not fond of speculating on market potential and would prefer to proceed immediately to the more concrete subject of annual sales.

In the case of existing products experience in the market will have helped to identify potential users and perhaps to separate immediate from ultimate potential. It is then a matter of putting a number to each category. Very often there are published statistics that will help. These may be produced by the government or by trade associations or may be quoted in trade journals. There are also private companies which publish lists of different types of businesses, perhaps subdivided by size or number of employees. Market research agencies naturally collect material of this kind for use in selecting samples for their surveys, although at this stage it may not be necessary to seek outside help. Some digging could be needed, but it is a job that could be undertaken by an intelligent and well-motivated junior, if proper briefing is given.

When contemplating a new market, definitions of ultimate and immediate potential are more speculative. It may be possible to use analogies with other industries, or with market experience in other countries, but caution is needed. Several mistakes have stemmed from a naive belief that what happened in the USA yesterday is about to happen in Europe tomorrow. It may well do so, but with differences that can make or break an enterprise.

The distinction between ultimate and immediate potential is especially important when experience of a market is limited. If it is assumed incorrectly that the ultimate potential is immediately available, and that the product is right for that ultimate potential, some real howlers can be made. It is perhaps invidious to select one out of many possible examples, but the Sinclair C5 electric 'vehicle' would be a classic, except that it probably had no potential of any kind, immediate or ultimate.

Penetration

Estimating penetration is a much less creative activity. It could be done by a field survey, but this would be an expensive way of finding out how many firms use a product, if that was all that was wanted. Often desk research will provide as accurate a picture as is required. Whether penetration is 30 per cent, say, or 35 per cent is usually of no great consequence, and field research would be unlikely to work to finer limits. What you want to know is whether penetration is in the region of 30 per cent, or in the region of something much greater or smaller.

Sometimes even if no estimates of penetration have been published, figures of sales have been. It is possible to add them together, so long as an allowance is made for replacement business. When the replacement component is not known it may be feasible to construct a model based on an assumed average life for each item after it has been sold. Sometimes, as when licences have to be obtained, exact figures are readily available, but usually a sensible estimate is the best that can be expected.

The important point about penetration, as with potential, is that it should receive thought, so that the sky is not assumed to be the limit, but some reasonable figures are compiled to show how far the market has yet to go. Past trends in annual sales can then be set against these figures and the future predicted more realistically than might otherwise be the case.

Annual sales

So much emphasis has traditionally been put on figures of total annual sales that it is not surprising to find that they are frequently quite easy to obtain. Trade journals may publish estimates at least and government figures for production and imports may be available. Sometimes however it is not so easy. Where no trade figures or official statistics exist, or where their reliability is suspect, it may be necessary to:

1 Build up total sales by estimating those of each competitor in turn (e.g. from published accounts or personal contacts).

2 Find a factor relating the product in question to others for which figures are available.

3 Conduct a field survey.

These methods are not of course mutually exclusive. For many industrial products the third course would be prohibitively expensive. This is because of the sample size needed for a survey into annual sales. Unless a market is very compact or completely saturated, it can be hard enough to locate users of any kind in sufficient quantity. To find those who bought last year rather than at some earlier date is harder still.

The first two methods used in combination can produce a better picture on many occasions. It is not always possible to find a factor which can be used, but if you try hard enough it is surprising how often something relevant turns up. It might be a component in the product which is rarely used for anything else, or it might be something of which the product itself is a component. An example may serve to illustrate this.

In the case study which forms Chapter 7, some research was commissioned into the market for balustrading. Balustrading is quite hard to define, because it can be taken to mean almost any form of railing. In this case the interest was in balustrading primarily associated with staircases. Even so it was not considered of great significance in the broad total of building costs, so no separate figures had been prepared or published. However statistics of output for the construction industry as a whole were available, broken down into sectors (factories, offices, warehouses, shops, etc.) and also into geographical regions.

The consultant conducting the research had had experience of the construction industry so he knew where to lay his hands on several hundred cost analyses of building projects. These showed the proportion of total costs that could be attributed to staircases. A smaller number gave balustrading as a proportion of overall staircase costs. So the consultant could make a calculation which showed balustrading as a factor of the total building output. Naturally the result was approximate, but it could be checked against the direct experience of the client company in instances where both the cost of balustrading and the value of the project of which it formed a part were known. It was accepted as providing a workable estimate of annual sales.

None of the methods suggested is without some possibility of error. In general this has to be accepted. There is however one classical error which should be avoided in compiling a total from the sales of known participants in the market. This is 'double counting'. Company A sells part of its output direct to the user, and part to Company B, which in turn sells to the ultimate customer. Sales figures are then obtained from both Company A and Company B. They are, let us assume, accurate in themselves, but when added they produce an inflated total if what we are looking for is sales to the end user. It is therefore necessary to be careful in calculating figures for any market in which there is a substantial amount of inter-trading between participants.

Competitors' shares

In a sense it would be good to have the 'double counting' problem to contend with. At least it means that figures for individual competitors are available. Often they are, but when this is not the case, an examination of published company accounts may help. These will of course give only a financial figure, not numbers of units sold or of orders taken. And where a company has more than one product it may not be easy to separate from the overall turnover that part which represents sales of the product in which you are interested.

When nothing else will serve a field survey should be able to determine without too much difficulty what proportion of customers are using the products of different competitors. These market shares are however 'historical'. Questions about the date of installation might make it possible to get a feel for the current position at the same time, but any conclusions based on this would probably have little statistical validity unless the sample were to be very large or the market very recent in origin.

Competitors' selling methods and pricing policies

In existing markets there should be ample information to hand about competitors' selling methods and pricing policies. The only difficulty lies in sifting the facts from a background of hearsay, which will contain an element of axe-grinding on the part of customers or sales representatives.

From outside a market it may not be so easy to make a realistic evaluation. Anything that is available through price lists, sales literature, press releases or advertisements will no doubt be studied. Sometimes however the sales approach adopted in the field and the prices actually charged are at variance with the published material. Furthermore, as we have seen, it is necessary to form a view not just of competitive behaviour now, but of competitive behaviour as it might be when we have launched our own attack upon the market.

A few interviews with customers and a closer look at competitors' accounts and financial structures may help to clarify the position. But where these issues are important a field survey could be desirable. Questions on competitors' selling methods can then be linked into an enquiry into the reaction of customers to the tactics adopted.

Customer buying motives

Motives can at times be hard to elucidate. We know the image that the company is trying to present and, when things go right, it is easy to assume that this is because customers have responded as predicted. When an order is lost, however, there is often some confusion about exactly why this has happened. Customers are in such circumstances reluctant to display their thought processes in full. Often it is easier to say that the price was too high, rather than that the product seemed inferior or that those selling it were completely ineffective.

Internal investigations and even discussions with the company's own customers are therefore likely to prove misleading. An in-depth survey of customer motivation is possible, but can be expensive because it involves personal interviews by highly qualified industrial interviewers. On the other hand it is comparatively simple to design a telephone questionnaire that will enable customers to rank various factors (delivery to time, product performance, information provided, technical assistance and so on) in order of importance, or to put forward their own reasons for buying. If this is administered without the interested company being identified, what emerges should be free of bias and could provide a broad guide to those aspects of the product or of its presentation that are of key importance.

Short of an in-depth interview it can be harder to determine customers' attitudes towards price. This is because price is not simply another factor to be listed and marked in order of importance. It has always to be set against a package of benefits. Would customers, for example, accept a lower level of reliability if price were to be reduced? Or would they be willing to pay more for improved performance? Such questions may be put, but the answers will always be suspect until customers are asked to pay real money for a specific package.

Customer buying practices

Who makes the buying decision may not be a question with a one-word reply. The name on an order, for instance, may be that of a professional buyer, while the actual decision to buy may have been taken on technical grounds by the works director. Sometimes a decision has to go through a series of people, and it is not necessarily the most senior who has the greatest influence. This is particularly the case where a decision is no longer about whether to buy but about a choice to make from among a number of competitive offerings. When contemplating a market of which the company has no previous experience a field survey can make clear what is normal practice, because questions can be asked directly about how the last purchase to be made was handled.

There are a number of other facets of buying that could be incorporated in the same enquiry, how orders are issued and on what terms, how payment is usually made, whether there are seasonal trends in purchasing. Most of these however can be established without a formal survey, even by a company approaching the market from outside.

Awareness and reputation

Up to now we have been looking wherever possible for ways of uncovering information needed without the cost of field research. When it comes to assessing awareness or checking the reputation of all participants in a given market there is no short cut, even for companies well established in that market. To balance this, it can be said that surveys directed at awareness and reputation are quick, effective and much cheaper than a full investigation into other quantitative and qualitative aspects of the market. They can also, in many cases, be extended to bring in other useful bits of information about, for example, customers' priorities in choosing a supplier, or their methods of acquiring information on what is available in the market. The result can be a low-cost study, of primary use in planning sales promotion and the selling approach, but with important implications for the factory or the service department in defining what customers really want.

Effective low-cost research

Even if research is to be carried out in-house, it starts with a clear *brief* of what is wanted. That is of course the questions to which the company is seeking answers, not to be confused with the questions appearing on the questionnaire itself. Let us suppose that you would like to know:

- who makes the buying decision
- what aspects of the product/service are rated most important
- how prospective customers know what is available
- what suppliers they are aware of
- how they rate suppliers (against a number of factors).

To complete a brief of this kind it will be necessary to define the universe you are addressing. Is it users or both users and non-users? Are they public authorities, water companies, plastics manufacturers, or what? Are there any size limits to those you want sampled (e.g. over 100 employees)? You will also need to define the aspects of the product that you want to investigate (durability, capacity, ease of operation, and so on), and the ways in which customers might learn what is available (advertisements, calls by representatives, exhibitions, third party recommendations, etc.). If advertising could be important, you might also compile a list of the media to which respondents might refer.

How many interviews?

The next decision to make is the number of respondents to be interviewed and how they will be approached. There is a choice of personal interviews, telephone interviews or postal questionnaires. They each have advantages and work well in given circumstances. This particular survey lends itself to telephone interviews. It is not seeking in-depth information, is concise and can be administered quickly. There could however be a combination of telephone and personal interviews, if it was desired to pursue some aspects in greater depth.

The number required, or feasible, depends partly on the type of interview chosen. Sheer cost usually restricts the number of personal interviews undertaken, for instance. Research agencies will usually quote for a fixed number of the type they recommend. It is however rare that that will be high enough to provide the statistical accuracy we have come to expect from, say, opinion polls. A thousand industrial interviews would cost a great deal; it is more likely that an agency will quote for 100 or 200 at the most. In practice that will probably suffice. If you are doing the research yourself it is not strictly necessary to fix a precise number in advance. This is because there is a way of knowing when sufficient interviews have been completed.

What is involved is a consistency test. You take the first batch of, say, 50 interview reports and analyse replies to a question of main importance. Suppose the finding was that 20 per cent used a certain product and 80 per cent did not. Then, when the next batch of 50 reports are ready, they are added to the first and the cumulative response analysed. Now the percentages might be 25 per cent and 75 per cent. You keep adding batches until the latest analysis does not vary by more than a few percentage points from the previous one. You can then assume that however many more interviews were to be conducted the response would not change significantly.

Statisticians have more complex ways of measuring consistency, but this one works. It is of course necessary to ensure that the universe is homogeneous and is sampled at random in a uniform way. I once failed to brief a young researcher on this point and found that she had taken her first batch from East Anglia and her second from the north of England. That is emphatically not the way to apply a consistency test. When we got it right in exercises of this kind, a consistent result could often be obtained from 100 to 150 interviews.

It cannot be assumed that the same accuracy will apply when the information is broken down into smaller cells. What is true of 100 interviews may be equally true of 10, but the possibility of statistical error is much greater. Any conclusions drawn from a cell of less than about 30 respondents should be treated with extreme caution. Conclusions based on the entire sample are to be preferred. So, if you want accuracy, keep the survey simple.

The questionnaire

Questionnaire design requires practice. Whether you want to try it yourself, or to look critically at a draft questionnaire prepared by someone else there are a few principles worth bearing in mind.

In the first place, if we are dealing with telephone interviews, the interviewer has to make sure that the right respondent has been obtained (normally the decision-maker) and explain the purpose of the call. An assurance has to be given that replies will be treated anonymously. It may also be necessary to reassure respondents that no sales approach will follow; and this must be absolutely true.

Early questions should be chosen both to create a logical sequence of enquiries and to avoid any tension at this stage of the interview. Resistance is still quite strong at the beginning of the substantive questionnaire, so any awkward questions should be left until later. Every question should be capable of being answered 'off the cuff'. If the respondent has to look for facts and figures, the interviewer is soon in trouble. Even in postal questionnaires or semi-structured personal interviews the principle of simplicity, of making it easy for the respondent to answer, should be observed, but in telephone interviews it is vital. If the telephone has to be put down, the interview may well end prematurely. In any case the whole conversation should not take longer than 5 or 10 minutes at the most. A lot of ground can be covered in that time.

That questions should not be framed in such a way that they point to specific answers is obvious enough. A glance at press reports of 'surveys' carried out by pressure groups or environmental bodies will indicate quite clearly what happens when this principle is breached. Now much of marketing also is directed towards persuasion rather than the search for truth, so no one should feel immune to the dangers of leading questions. It is for this reason, among others, that market research is better kept quite separate from the activities of sales people or advertising agents.

In some instances it is possible to obtain an unprompted response before giving your respondent assistance in answering the question. 'What suppliers do you know of in this field?' might produce one or two names only, but these are valuable because they were in the forefront of the customer's mind. 'I have a list of names here, can you tell me if any are familiar to you?' could easily result in more names, because the memory has been jogged. That is also a valid research finding, but it would be better to seek unprompted responses first. If a list of names is quoted it should be in a random order that does not imply any form of priority. When it has to be used for a second time the order can be changed. It is possible, if there are doubts about the replies to a prompted question (where, for example, overall awareness is believed to be very low) to include a non-existent company name as a check.

A pilot survey

Whether you are conducting a postal or a telephone survey – or indeed personal interviews – a pilot survey is essential. You may think you have been crystal clear in the questions asked, but there is only one way to find out. The advantage of telephone interviews is that this takes only a day or two. When problems are diagnosed, or bad reactions encountered, it is necessary to think again, and to conduct another pilot if the changes are other than minor. With a telephone survey my own experience is that a pilot of 10 or 12 interviews will be sufficient to throw up any major problems.

Analysis

When all the replies are in and you are happy about their consistency a final analysis can be made. Many research companies use computers for this or give the donkey work to junior staff. This can be quite satisfactory if the analysis is closely supervised. In small surveys of the kind we are looking at, I have always preferred to do the analysis myself, by hand. It is laborious, but it puts flesh on the bare statistics and enables a 'feel' to be given even where the numbers involved are too small for firm conclusions.

In any case, however the analysis is made, a debriefing session with the interviewers is a must. Their overall impressions can be worth gathering, and at the same time, by talking with them you will be in a better position to interpret what they have written on the report forms. Naturally the debriefing should take place as soon as possible on completion of the survey.

Could you do it yourself?

A survey of the sort outlined here needs a clear brief, a sampling list, trained interviewers, good questionnaire design and competent analysis. There is no reason why it could not be done in-house. To preserve anonymity interviewers should work from outside the company, but that is really the only snag. If in any doubt, however, have a survey done by an independent research consultant or agency, and take a keen interest in the mechanics of what is done. Even if, after that, you feel that you cannot afford the time and dedication needed to conduct your own research, you will still benefit from a more discerning insight into the methods used by others.

Ethics

For those who set out to do their own research, there are rules to be observed. No respondent must be identified. Using an outside agency ensures this. If you do it yourself provision has to be made for the security of interview reports. Normal practice is to destroy them after two years or so. This could be done earlier, once it is clear that there are no more queries on the results, but until reports are destroyed they must be kept under lock and key, and right away from anyone on the sales side of the company.

It has been assumed that no one will attempt to use the sales force for market research: this would be most unfair to sales people. They have a job to do in obtaining orders, and that job does not consort easily with the task of market research. Should they succeed in changing roles and adopting a completely objective approach, their company affiliations would still be known to customers, influencing replies in quite unpredictable ways.

Market acceptance tests

Sales help may be useful in setting up interviews for market acceptance tests, where often there is no point in anonymity. Objectivity is however just as important as in other forms of research. In the example given in Chapter 1 respondents were shown a number of different telephone instruments to get their reactions. As shape was the issue, not colour, they were all produced in the same colour, and placed in a display case in such a way that no obvious order of preference could be inferred. In Chapter 7 we shall see some simpler acceptance tests, where the interviewer is accompanied by a salesman. The salesman however, leaves all the questions to the interviewer and neither of them displays in any way his own personal view of the products on show.

Wider surveys

As has been argued much quantitative market information can be acquired by desk research or intelligent enquiry, blended with an imaginative approach to related facts and figures that can be used to throw light on the market in which you are interested. There are limits to what can be done in-house. Industrial research often makes good use of interviews with competitors. These can be difficult if not impossible when you are a competitor yourself or are proposing to become one. They are not easy for agencies either, but an established agency can often gain access to competitors who will be interested in talking about the market, and will be hoping to gain a little knowledge in return. The interviewers used for this work are the best in the business, and are far more likely than you or I to emerge with useful information.

Research agencies may also have access to facts and figures not readily obtainable by their clients. In the case study described in Chapter 7, this, and the greater resources an agency had for a widespread survey, was enough to tip the balance in favour of seeking outside help. Large-scale research needs to be in the hands of an organization that can cope with all aspects of it, from desk research to interviews of all types.

The choice of an agency

In commissioning an agency there is a choice between those that specialize in consumer research and those that concentrate on industrial or business to business work. It is rare to find one that handles both types of work equally well. As we are here concerned with industrial marketing it may seem that there is no decision to make. Nevertheless consumer agencies could be well equipped to handle such matters as market acceptance tests. They will almost certainly have more experience of this type of work than industrial research firms.

In either field there are a limited number of companies with an established reputation. The best way to find one suited to what you have in mind is through recommendation. It is also worthwhile consulting the *Market Research Society's Yearbook* or its list of *Organisations and Individuals Providing Market Research Services.*[1] When two or three agencies have been selected which seem to fit your requirements, they can be visited to get an idea of their approach to your assignment, and to look at the resources and people they can deploy. It is important to identify the person who is actually going to do your research. Some agencies have senior executives who will take your brief, prepare a quotation and then hand over to a comparatively inexperienced junior.

Quotations cannot be compared on grounds of price alone, or even by comparing costs per interview. You do however want to know how many interviews are proposed, and of what type. What really matters is the skill with which the whole exercise will be carried out,

[1]Both available from the Market Research Society, 15 Northburgh Street, London.

and the more you know yourself about research methods, the better you will be able to judge this. One aspect that should be looked at closely is whether you are being presented with a standardized approach or whether the agency has studied *your* requirements in detail. It is also worth noting whether you are told without asking, not only what information the agency aims to provide but exactly how it intends to obtain it.

Such attention to a client's specific needs cannot be expected of a *syndicated survey*. Surveys of this type usually cover a whole industry and offer to subscribers a mix of quantitative and qualitative information. By spreading charges over a number of clients they reduce the cost to participants. The fact that the information is given to others with whom you are competing should not worry any competent marketor unduly. Indeed if it serves to make the policies adopted by competitors more realistic, this could be for the benefit of the industry in general. It may even be possible to get questions to which you want specific answers included in surveys of this kind. Close scrutiny of the credentials and methods of the research organization is just as important with syndicated as with individual surveys if you are to get value for money.

Questions and action points for decision takers

Attitudes to research

What market research has been conducted on behalf of the company?

What happened as a result of it?

If research has been proposed and rejected, why was that?

Are there entrenched attitudes hostile to research?

The scope of market research

Do you have for each product an *objective* assessment of:

- potential: ultimate and immediate
- penetration to date
- annual sales (all competitors combined)
- new and replacement components of sales
- trends in total sales
- competitors' shares of sales
- trends in competitors' shares
- competitors' selling methods
- competitors' pricing policies
- customer buying motives
- customer buying practices
- awareness and reputation of the company
- product trends
- market threats and opportunities?

Uses of research

If so, how is the information used in:

- strategic planning
- design and development

- production
- installation and service
- financial planning
- the sales force
- sales promotion?

Research methods

If further information is needed will it be obtained by:

- desk research
- use of analogies
- field survey
- a combination of these methods?

Planning the research

Do you have a clear brief of the research required?

Can it be done in-house?

Can any field research needed be kept simple?

If it can, and can be done in-house:

- who will control it?
- how will interviews be conducted?
- what provisions will be made for
  —a pilot survey
  —consistency tests?
- how will the analysis be made?
- who will write the report?
- what steps are planned to protect the anonymity of respondents?

Choice of an agency

If an outside agency is needed:

- who will vet the choice of agency?
- are the agency's proposals tailored to your requirements?

- has the agency explained in detail how the job will be done?

Are there any syndicated surveys available as a low-cost alternative?

7

The acid test

Integration in launching a new product

It is time to look at integration in the round. To define the concept we have had to examine, department by department, the scope that exists for integration and the obstacles that lie in its path. But in practice everything happens at once, throughout the company and along with a host of unrelated matters which demand urgent attention. That in itself is no cause for apprehension, if the foundations of an integrated approach are already in place. It merely reflects the conditions under which business operates. At this stage it might be useful to take an example from the recent history of one firm, to see just how easy or difficult it may have been to make integrated marketing work.

The example chosen is not one of spectacular success. The firm is small and the product modest, both in itself and in the level of sales achieved. Yet for this very reason it may be possible to see more clearly what is going on. There is an air of unreality about the great success stories of marketing. You know from experience that there must have been a large element of luck, or at least of being in the right place at the right time, yet it is often presented by those involved, or their admirers, as the culmination of a masterly plan or a stroke of marketing genius. If that were indeed the case, there is little hope that ordinary mortals could learn anything from it, because genius cannot be reproduced at will.

What we are looking for is something less ambitious. It is evidence that the integration of marketing effort is both feasible and beneficial; that it can lead to the attainment of the level of competence necessary for survival and hopefully for growth in really tough, competitive markets. I have chosen to illustrate the launch of a new product in a firm in the construction industry. It was a good test of the degree of marketing integration that had been achieved at the time and of the extent to which that had to be improved to meet the challenge of a launch of this nature. No attempt has been made to gloss over the mistakes that occurred. It is all recent history and those involved are still absorbing the lessons learned. I am, of course, one of those involved.

Background: the need for a new product

The company

J. Starkie Gardner Limited was founded in 1752. The company has always had as its main product architectural metalwork, but the nature of that product has changed over the years. Iron gates, ornamental work and statues have been replaced by high quality balustrading and staircases. This reflected changes in the market and culminated, in 1969, with a move from London to Hadleigh in Suffolk. In the course of this the forge, which had been the company's pride, was relinquished in favour of bending, welding and polishing machinery suitable for handling stainless steel, brass or aluminium railings and balusters.

Product range

By 1980 the range consisted of balustrading for feature staircases and concourses, mainly custom-built to the designs of various architects. The balustrading in which the company specialized included 'structural glass', where the handrail is connected to the stair or floor by glass panels and the glass forms an integral part of the strength of the structure, as well as more conventional arrangements with vertical metal balusters or horizontal intermediate rails. Materials could be mixed, with handrails in, say, timber and balusters made of brass. Everything depended on the architect's requirement. The drawing office had to interpret this in a way which was practicable for the site in question.

In addition to handling one-off projects of this kind Starkie Gardner offered a balustrading *system*, under the trade mark 'Strading'. The key element in Strading was an aluminium handrail, slotted on the underside, into which balusters of a number of different designs could be fixed wherever desired. It was a medium-priced product, but carried a good profit margin because both handrail and balusters were standardized and could be stocked, while drawing office costs were lower and fixing on site presented few problems.

The market

Enquiries were received from architects and contractors. An architect would always specify the materials to be used and sometimes would nominate a particular supplier. More often the requirement was stated in general terms and buying decisions were made by contractors who would receive tenders from a number of potential suppliers. The projects with which they were concerned ranged from public buildings to shopping centres, offices, industrial sites and, very occasionally, high-class housing developments. The majority of the work was new construction although there was an element of refurbishment.

Most orders were in the form of contracts common throughout the construction industry. These enabled the main contractor to pass on to subcontractors and suppliers very heavy penalties in the event of a failure to perform to time. Main contractors were also able, outside the terms of the contract, to postpone payment for a variety of reasons, if given the slightest excuse to do so. From the point of view of the supplier this made it a very tough market indeed, and one where great care had to be exercised in tendering for and accepting orders, and in managing contracts efficiently. The advantage in any dispute was all on the side of the large contractor against a generally much smaller supplier.

Competition

There were a number of companies offering a range of products at the top end of the market. Most of these were quite small with a turnover of £1 500 000 to £2 500 000 a year and with perhaps 40 to 70 employees.

Two or three competitors were offering balustrading systems of various types and appeared to be operating at about the same level in terms of sales volume. In the broader market for cheaper balustrading and external railings the competition was any firm out of hundreds that could weld or bend mild steel.

Recent history

From what has been said it will be clear that small companies in this field are highly vulnerable. A serious miscalculation at an awkward moment can prove fatal. In 1984 Starkie Gardner paid the price of a series of errors and fell into receivership. The company was purchased by a Cambridge firm manufacturing spiral staircases. The price was low and a potentially valuable asset had been acquired. The production and marketing of standard spirals is however very different from the business of handling the much larger projects in which Starkie Gardner was involved. Attempts to run the newly bought subsidiary from the management resources available at Cambridge put a strain on both companies and forced a radical re-think.

This was the point at which I got to know Starkie Gardner. A group of consultants called Management in Action, who were advising the parent organization, asked me to take charge of the company at Hadleigh. The brief was to put the business firmly back on the rails and to look for a permanent successor to take over as soon as possible. This was in September 1985. It was hoped by the Cambridge board of directors that a new managing director could be appointed early in 1986. The current production director, Harry Watson, was not held responsible for the circumstances that had brought about receivership and was considered to be a candidate for the job. One of my tasks was to make a firm assessment of his capabilities.

The details of this early phase need not concern us unduly. Measures taken included getting a firm grip on cash flow and revising pricing policy to enhance the company's chances of securing the type of business it could handle most profitably. It was obvious that additional changes were needed to improve the firm's marketing capability. While I was looking at these Harry Watson was setting up a planned production programme to ensure that deliveries and installation would be on time.

To my great relief management accounts were already in good order, and comparable to those of many larger organizations. Detailed figures of expenditure for all departments were prepared monthly and invoicing could be predicted for several weeks in advance. Harry and I devised additional returns and analyses which enabled us to measure the profitability of each project, to calculate the conversion rates for quotations made for each type of product, and so on. There was no money available at this stage for market research, but a close examination of the facts and figures produced internally enabled us to bid for the business that would do the company most good and reject anything that might over-extend our embryonic management team.

By January 1986 I was satisfied that the company was working on a sound basis and was glad to hand over to Harry Watson, who was appointed managing director. From then on my role was purely advisory. The day-to-day operations of the company gave no cause for concern. Turnover rose from £460 000 for the year ending September 1985 to £1 280 000 in 1985–86. The year end accounts once more showed a profit. There were however a number of strategic issues looming on the horizon if the company was to grow to the £3 000 000 level which everyone felt should be the longer term objective.

Problems of growth

A prime difficulty was contract management. If the company was going to expand volume in custom-built projects for feature balustrading, the pressure this would bring on the man in charge had to be considered. Whoever was delegated to handle the details, when arguments arose between the company and a main contractor, the contractor would insist on talking to the managing director. This meant that Harry Watson might well have to travel to site, or at least field telephone queries from the contractor's high-powered project management team. To be involved in the details of such jobs was not hobbyism: it was a condition of being paid. We suspected that it was for this, as much as for any other reason, that the sales of our competitors struggled to go far beyond £2 000 000 a year. There were simply limits to the number of custom-built jobs that one man could handle as the market demanded.

A study of competitors' annual accounts lent weight to this consideration. Both turnover and profit seemed to fluctuate quite wildly. This was especially the case where really large contracts were known to have been accepted. It seemed that they absorbed almost all of a company's efforts until suddenly they were completed and a scramble followed to fill production slots left vacant. Indeed it would be strange if large contracts and small companies meshed easily together.

So what were our options? The marketing and administration costs of obtaining many small contracts to smooth production and ease the burden on top management were excessive. Medium-sized custom-built projects looked attractive, but a £50 000 contract could involve a great deal of management. In general there was no reason to feel that four at £50 000 were preferable to one at £200 000, and the marketing effort was certainly going to be greater if four were needed.

One possible solution appeared to lie in the further development of balustrading systems. 'Strading' had been bringing in about £100 000 a year. If this could be increased substantially it could produce orders that did not require constant attention from top management. Strading was profitable even if individual orders were taken at a lower value than most custom-built projects.

Two decisions were taken at this time. One was to commission a market survey which it was hoped would quantify the market as a whole and its main sectors, and indicate the scope for growth across the company's range of products. The other was to look at ways of increasing systems business. Nothing that the market survey was likely to reveal was going to invalidate that course of action, considering the current low level of sales.

Son of Strading

The attempt to find an improved version of Strading or something to take its place began quite early in 1986. No one at the time commented on the difficulty of pursuing a dual objective of this kind. The thinking processes that lead to improvements to existing products are very different from those which discard past and present and look for something altogether new. What is more, one type of thinking will almost certainly inhibit the other.

A meeting was held with the aim of stimulating ideas for a new product with the advantages of standardization that a system could bring. It was attended by the chief designer, estimators and the company's two sales representatives. The procedures of a 'brainstorming' session were followed meticulously. All that was wanted was ideas, any ideas, and criticism of anything put forward was reserved for a later date. I had run sessions of this kind many times and was quite confident that in the relaxed atmosphere prevailing something useful would emerge; but for the first hour there was an unprecedented degree of silence. Afterwards we came, perhaps unfairly, to think of this as a 'Suffolk' brainstorming. There was no rush to produce bright ideas, but rather a series of murmurs and grunts, while hands scribbled, apparently idly, on pieces of paper.

At the end of the day it was clear that what was on the paper was not just doodling but sketches of alternative versions of the product. There had been no lack of will or effort. It was just that some of the people concerned thought with their fingers rather than their tongues. There had however been an inhibiting factor present. This was the difficulty of escaping from the design concept of the existing Strading system. So what emerged in the end was an augmentation of Strading, rather than a new product.

The two most likely lines of approach seemed to be a new, tubular handrail and the promotion of colour as a feature. Samples were made and later in 1986 I went with one of our representatives to visit architects and get reactions. The response was not unfavourable but hardly enthusiastic. It was clear that 'Son of Strading' was unlikely to make a sufficient contribution to the company's expansion, and that we needed to think again.

A market survey

Early in 1987 the results of our market survey became available. It had not been easy to measure the size of the market because of a certain vagueness in the definition of the term 'balustrading'. Nevertheless it was large and the company's share of the overall total of annual sales was around 5 per cent. With a market growing at 4 per cent per annum this left plenty of scope for expansion, even when it was calculated that our share of balustrading made from the higher quality materials was more like 11 per cent.

Awareness of the company among architects and contractors was reasonably high. In fact we were listed second in the table of competitors. It was however thought significant that the firm with the highest level of awareness was one which imported a system from Germany and sold no custom-built balustrading at all. At the time we were inclined to attribute this to heavier sales promotion, but later evidence suggests that where awareness ratings rather than reputation ratings are concerned, the linking of a name to a specific product or system helps to create a clearer identity. In any event the research findings could only encourage us to look for a new system while continuing to expand our market share in the high-quality custom-built sector.

The origins of STARGARD

Naturally there had been thoughts of expanding into new markets as well as of increasing our share in the United Kingdom. The first step in this had been to investigate the Dutch and German markets. Apart from desk research and contacts with possible installers and distributors this had involved visiting a few exhibitions, to see what competition there was, and to evaluate the prospects for offering Strading or custom-built balustrading in either of these countries.

It was on a visit that Harry and I made in February 1987 to Bouwbeurs at Utrecht that two items caught our attention. One was a transparent acrylic handrail. The other was a rail coated with thick PVC providing a matt, coloured finish with a warm feel to it which had standardized aluminium fittings so that it constituted something like a system. Instead of finding a market for our own existing products, we had found some of the ideas our brainstorming had failed to provide.

By May I was ready to conduct some research among architects, armed with samples of both the transparent rail, which I felt to be most attractive, and the PVC coated rail, a much more utilitarian product. The results were quite unequivocal. There was little or no interest in my beautiful acrylic rail, and very considerable enthusiasm for the PVC coated rail.

We decided to market the PVC coated system and considered whether to import it or manufacture it ourselves. From the outset there was no question of complete manufacture in Holland, because this was not an entirely standardized system. Rails had to be cut and shaped to order. There were discussions on the possibility of importing the fittings only and making the rails locally, but the cost of shipping the components was high and in the end it was mutually decided that neither company would benefit much from a deal. It would be simpler for us to manufacture the complete balustrade in Hadleigh. So a development programme was started.

Development

The intention was to offer a system which combined custom-built elements with standard railings and fittings. In this way it was felt that one of the company's strengths, its ability to make to order, would be employed against well-entrenched competition. There would also be an advantage in minimizing the number of visible joins. With a completely standardized system there had to be many joins to get the rails around bends and corners without shaping them individually.

Our chief competitor offered a system of excellent quality, but consisting entirely of standard lengths and bends. It was made of hard, shiny plastic, injection-moulded on to metal tube, in a range of bright primary colours. To assemble it on site, pieces were joined together mechanically, so that there were frequent right-angled bends and many joins. The total effect was neat enough and its modernity appealed to many architects. Against this we meant to bend rails to suit individual sites, then coat them with plastic. The PVC coating was available as a tube which was heated, then drawn on to the pre-shaped metal rail. The finished product is illustrated in Figure 7.1 which gives an indication of how the handrail was fitted to the balusters and how glass infill panels were attached when they formed part of the design.

Other ideas were built into the product specification at this time which had serious consequences. It was thought that by using

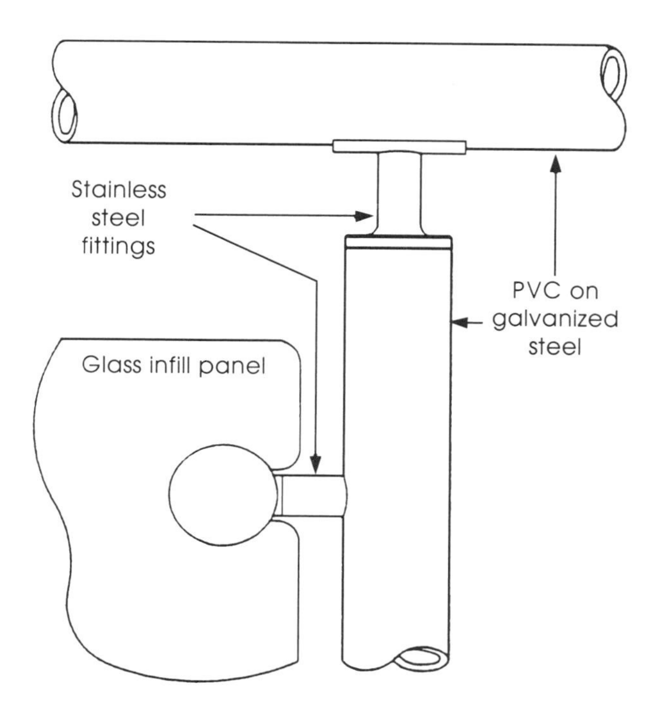

Figure 7.1 STARGARD: the finished design

galvanized rail and making the fittings of stainless steel rather than aluminium a system could be produced that could be used both internally and externally. In addition the stainless steel fittings looked much smarter than the aluminium version. Everyone who saw the prototype felt that the system looked *right*.

What was not fully appreciated was the effect of this on cost. The earliest estimates indicated that we might be able to offer something that could compete on price with nylon-coated mild steel, a superior form of paint finish. That would have placed the product at the top of the lower-priced sector of the market. The improvements now made removed any possibility of this, because no sooner had the design been settled than the price of stainless steel surged upward.

Is this another example of the engineering attrition discussed in Chapter 1? Certainly it has many of the characteristics noted there. It is also true that no one seriously queried the decision to go ahead with stainless steel and not revert to something cheaper. Is this because, in its usual subtle way, engineering attrition had spread an aura of inevitability about something that was in fact a matter of simple choice? By moving the product out of the lower end of the market and placing it firmly in the middle it is possible that we restricted sales. Yet no marketing voice was raised against the chosen design. Perhaps this was because realization of the cost implications of the decision came slowly, as the price of stainless steel increased. But by then the reception that customers gave to the product had reinforced a general belief that it was right for its job, and so it remained firmly in the mid-priced area.

A separate unit

During 1987 the overall business had been expanding rapidly enough to create worries about the space available. With a new product under development, problems were foreseen unless extra accommodation could be obtained. To cater for this a small industrial unit, about a quarter of a mile from the main factory, was taken on a short-term rental.

Of course there was no necessity to put the new product into this unit. Some other department could have moved there to free space in the factory. Nevertheless there seemed to be much in favour of locating everything to do with the new venture there. Harry Watson believed that to market a systems product effectively demanded a change in thinking. Deliveries had to be shorter and communication between those responsible for selling, estimating, design and production had to be more effective.

It was decided to create a miniature business in the new unit. One of the company's two salesmen was located there along with sufficient people to get the project off the ground, and an ambitious young man was employed to take overall responsibility. In the meantime efforts were to be made to convert existing enquiries into orders for the new product, so that field trials could be made. By mid-1988 the building was occupied and the new manager installed.

Choosing a name

Further brainstorming had taken place to find a name. As might have been expected from our first use of the technique, this proved that the company's skills were of a practical rather than a literary nature. It was however ultimately agreed by all that STARGARD represented the character of the product reasonably well, without being overtly descriptive. The name also chimed with thoughts we were having about market segmentation.

Market segmentation

Early analysis of the type of end-user for Starkie Gardner's balustrading had produced no clear picture. Whenever end-users could be identified it seemed that the company was serving a cross-section of British commerce and industry. Anywhere where a staircase was a feature of the design of a building rather than an escape route or 'tradesmen's entrance' qualified as a suitable site. It did however seem that public buildings such as schools, hospitals, council offices or old people's homes were under-represented. STARGARD with its warm, non-slip grip, its durability and its inherent strength seemed right for applications in the public sector. It was considered that this should be a prime target area at the launch of the product.

Initial marketing efforts

Sales forecasts

Overall turnover had increased from £1 280 000 in 1985–86 to

£1 500 000 in 1986–87 and was set to exceed £2 000 000 for the year ending September 1988. As outlined earlier there were reasons for doubting the ability of the company to handle much more than £2 500 000 in custom-built projects. Further expansion would have to come from systems products, Strading and STARGARD. Hopes of increasing Strading sales much beyond £100 000 were not high, but it was believed that STARGARD could reach £350 000 in the first full year of marketing, and that this figure might ultimately be doubled. The market appeared to offer scope for this in the public sector where there had been little participation previously and also in the private sector, from a spread of customers who might want something attractive in the medium-priced range.

Field trials

Much as expected, the site for our field trial was an old people's home. The salesman concerned and the manager of the STARGARD unit worked closely together to see that this was a success, but inevitably there were problems. The plastic covering, cut to match the inner steel tube tended to pull away at the joints, while drilling holes through both plastic and metal also created difficulties. None of the problems had been foreseen, but fortunately all were curable. As an example, in cutting rails before despatch to site, the plastic covering was allowed to overlap the metal tube, to be trimmed back during installation to make a neat joint.

In the course of a few weeks the lessons of the field trial had been digested, so that by the time the product was in full production everyone felt confident that it would do its job. The cost of early installations was however more than anticipated. It was assumed that much of this was due to the problems met and to inexperience in both manufacturing and installation. The corollary was that with time and greater volume, production would become more efficient, and costs would be reduced. But whatever extra efficiency was obtained, and in spite of a good deal of pressure from Harry Watson, STARGARD remained more expensive than originally anticipated. The prime cause of this was, of course, the rise in the cost of stainless steel. Whether this had a serious impact on sales is a matter of conjecture, since the only alternative would have been an inferior, though cheaper, product. The lingering belief that costs would come down did however have some unfortunate consequences.

Sales literature

In the balustrading market sales literature is an essential component of the marketing mix. Architects need to see the product, so good illustrations are worth more than glowing words. Technical details, along with references to any relevant standards, are also required. Larger architects' practices will maintain libraries in which product information is filed under a universal reference code.

Launching a new product poses problems when faced with these requirements. Pictures of completed installations are simply not available, and sketches and diagrams do not carry the same impact as finished work. In its turn the pre-eminence of visual aspects tends to make the preparation of literature appear as a hunt for suitable pictures, in the course of which consideration of its specific purpose and objectives may become blurred. Fortunately in this instance the fact that the company was addressing specific sectors of the market for the first time in its history made it both essential and possible to curb impatience and create a proper literature brief. This was given to a freelance designer, along with copy stressing what were believed to be STARGARD's main benefits. The one completed installation we had – that used for our field trial – was pictured as widely as possible, along with sample lengths of balustrading constructed especially for the leaflet.

By September 1988 all was ready for the launch. We felt confident that we had a good product and that our sales aids, literature and samples, were adequate. Unknown to everyone however one error of judgement had been made. Because of the belief that costs would come down once production was in full swing, too much emphasis had been placed on economy as a benefit. The original leaflet contained a claim that the product would be available at 'about the cost of powder-coated mild steel'. This was never achieved, although the differential in some cases was quite small.

Sales promotion: cost and enquiries

The product was launched through a combination of press advertising in trade journals, press releases issued by a freelance PR specialist and a direct mail campaign to local authorities and leading architects. The total cost in the first year from September 1988 was about £15 000. This brought in 3500 requests for literature and 190 firm enquiries for projects.

In the second year of the new product promotional expense was reduced to £6000. It seemed reasonable to make some reduction because it was felt that the momentum gained would not need as much to sustain it as had been spent on the initial launch. The extent of the reduction was a matter of judgement. In the event it may have been about right. Requests for literature fell to 1300, almost pro rata to promotional expense, but firm project enquiries rose to 240.

The effect of advertising

It was possible to make comparisons between the response to advertisements for STARGARD and the response to similar-sized advertisements for feature staircase balustrading placed in the same journal. In every instance publicizing an identifiable system brought substantially more requests for literature than promoting an all-round ability to handle quality work. A reputation for craftsmanship might prove durable – the firm enquiries received on a regular basis with or without advertising indicated that this was the case – but linking a specific product to the company name brought a much greater immediate response than advertising craftsmanship in general.

This finding confirmed the impression received from the formal market survey conducted previously. We had at the time been struck by the higher awareness rating given to a systems competitor. That this should have exceeded the ratings of several first-class companies competing at the top end of the custom-built market was now seen not simply as the result of high advertising expenditure but as an effect of combining advertising with a clear product identity.

With statistics for two full years to hand it was possible to reach a further conclusion. Initially it had been hard to relate the number of firm enquiries received to advertising. What an advertisement produced in the first instance was requests for literature, not firm enquiries. In time it became clear that some surge in project enquiries could be expected two or three months after the appearance of an advertisement. Such a surge was limited in its extent and its duration. Without continued advertising firm enquiries were still received, but on a declining scale.

There was no evidence that an enhanced advertising programme, reverting to the frequency of the launch period, would produce a commensurate return. Enquiries seemed to be coming in at a steady rate, as they did for other products. The difference was that to keep the rate steady for STARGARD required an occasional 'shot in the arm'. So advertising of systems products was seen as more volatile both in its immediate results and in the duration of its effect on business.

Success and its associated problems

Conversion of enquiries into orders

In the first year of operation 16 per cent of firm enquiries became orders. That compared favourably with the conversion ratio for most other products. One of the difficulties of the balustrading market is the comparatively low proportion of enquiries which become orders. The net value of the orders obtained in that year was £319 000. Although this was short of the £350 000 we had hoped to see it was considered to be a satisfactory start.

The second year not only saw more firm enquiries, but produced a higher conversion rate: 22 per cent of enquiries became orders, and sales volume rose to £373 000. The only cause for concern was that, had the value of each order been the same as it was on average in the previous year a total of well over £500 000 would have been expected. At the time the cause of the reduction in size of order was not clear. With hindsight it can be seen as the beginning of a malaise that was to affect the entire construction industry.

Noises off

No business activity happens in a vacuum. Within the company and outside a great deal was going on which would impinge on STARGARD. By September 1989 overall turnover had reached £2 200 000 and was still rising. By then also the parent company had been absorbed into a somewhat larger group, still in the construction industry. One result of this was that interest in expansion overseas waned, along with thoughts of the movement to larger premises that this would have necessitated.

If the company was to continue to grow within the space available to it internal efficiency had to improve. Pressures from the market-place on price, delivery and quality, and the availability of new computerized methods all pointed in the same direction. There was no way in which staffing levels and overheads could be allowed to grow in line with turnover.

The drawing office was one of the first places to receive attention, by the introduction of computer aided design. Similarly computers were brought in to the estimating department to speed the preparation of quotations. In either case STARGARD would have been an obvious candidate for all the new computer systems. The semi-standardized nature of the product lent itself to these methods. But STARGARD was not there to be computerized, because the entire operation was in a separate unit some distance away.

The reforms did not stop at computers. New production, buying and stock-keeping routines were introduced. A contracts manager was employed to take some of the burden off Harry Watson, and tighter contract controls were applied. Then the decision was made to apply for approval to BS 5750 Part 1. This was a quality standard which in our case applied to all aspects of balustrading design and manufacture. Every move that was in hand at that time implied a standardization of internal procedures. The STARGARD operation stood awkwardly apart from this, but in any case had been developing problems of its own.

Problems of isolation

Sales had increased, but not of course at a steady pace that allowed production in the small independent plant to be planned on an even basis. What had served admirably as a development unit failed to meet the peaks and troughs that intermittent ordering brought with it. Support from the main factory was needed in buying and storing materials and in inspecting goods received. Some drawing had to be done in the main drawing office as well, simply because of the volume of work on hand at any given time.

To have catered for all these activities within the STARGARD unit would have needed a disproportionate overhead structure. But once independence was seen as illusory morale began to fall. Originally members of a small team had worked well together in getting the product off the ground. Now they had to relate to other people who had different priorities. Strains became apparent between members of the team and managers in the main factory and drawing office, and were echoed within the team itself. Eventually both the unit manager and the salesman dedicated to STARGARD left the company to seek their fortunes elsewhere.

There was nothing for it but to bring the product back into the main factory, and this was done during 1990. Overcrowding was eased by a reorganization of the layout of the workshop. Once the production manager had accepted full responsibility for

STARGARD, problems began to fade. Harry Watson had to insist on faster drawing and production times for systems products, but this too was accepted when it was seen that these products offered some protection against the recession that was clearly deepening throughout the industry.

On the sales side too there were benefits to be gained. It had already been found that, while an assault on specific market sectors had paid dividends, there was still a wide area of application throughout commerce and industry. Wherever good quality was required but budget considerations precluded stainless steel or brass, STARGARD offered a possible solution. Our second salesman had therefore to become adept in STARGARD. He very soon showed himself to be at least as competent as the original specialist. The estimators also were able to select the enquiries for which STARGARD was suitable and work in close liaison with the salesman.

It is not easy to say whether a unified approach, with no separate unit, would have been more effective from the start. What had happened was as much the result of success as of failure. It was interesting that a fully integrated operation on a small scale worked well, and only seemed to falter when that integration was broken and problems of separation became apparent.

The third year

The year 1990 was crucial for the construction industry, and for Starkie Gardner. Because the fitting of balustrading comes late in the construction process the company still had plenty of work in hand. Output was above £2 700 000 and the production programme full for months ahead. Orders were however becoming harder to obtain.

Enquiries had begun to decline in 1989. By 1990 this had been reflected in orders, which were not only fewer but of smaller average size. What had been noticed in the second year of STARGARD was now universal for all orders. The situation worsened in 1991. Industry figures estimated that what had been a steady growth rate of 4 per cent in the past was due to become a decline of 40 per cent.

In spite of this and of the internal problems that had affected STARGARD and caused its production to be relocated in the main factory, orders had fallen only slightly in number: from 43 in the year ending September 1990 to 40 in the third year of operation. But the value of orders had been reduced to £262 000. Without the market collapse that had taken place this figure might well have been over £400 000 but that is a matter of speculation. In reality we had suffered a set-back in which the one bright spot was the improvement in the conversion ratio of orders from enquiries to 24 per cent.

A candle in the dark

The recession which had been expected to last only a year or two continued into 1992 and deepened. Turnover at Starkie Gardner peaked and then declined. By the end of 1992 orders were being received at a rate equivalent to little more than £1 200 000 in a full year. Competitors of good repute were sliding into financial difficulty if not insolvency. Every month brought news of a disaster somewhere in the industry.

As the market declined so the demands of customers became more insistent. Margins were of course under pressure, but faster delivery was also a key factor in obtaining orders. Everyone in the company became aware of what was needed to survive. The management systems which had been introduced earlier now paid a dividend. Estimating and drawing times were reduced, while manufacturing reaped the benefit of improved quality procedures. Attitudes underwent a radical change. Samples, which had been seen as an interruption to the workshop routine, were now produced in the knowledge that without them there might be no workshop.

Large, custom-built orders were still vital to the company's survival, but they were few and far between. And it was here that STARGARD, and to a lesser extent Strading, made a major contribution. The sales volume of these products was not so severely affected, and a steady stream of orders came in to help smooth production and maintain employment. Furthermore this was profitable business which contributed materially to maintaining cash flow. More important still was its effect on morale, STARGARD stood as a symbol of success, even when its original target had been consigned to the waste-bin.

The impact on Strading

One of the worries we had had in launching STARGARD had been the impact it might have on Strading. To some extent the two products might be seen as competitive. It was feared that pushing one might restrict sales of the other. Even where products have no direct relationship to one another it is common to find that sales effort switches to something new while older, established products suffer from neglect. This effect is one of the inherent dangers of launching any new product, but here we had two systems products, not too far from each other in price.

Strading turned out to be a remarkably stable product. Just as our efforts to increase sales with colour and new handrails had brought only a small return, so vigorous promotion of STARGARD appeared to have little adverse effect. The conversion ratio of Strading was high and stayed between 30 and 34 per cent throughout the first three years of STARGARD. Sales remained steady at about £100 000 a year. The recession made no impression at all. If ever there was a niche market it was Strading.

There was naturally a lesson in this beyond the obvious point that we had two products appealing to two different sectors of the market. The company's policy had always been to offer as far as possible the right product for each individual project. It might not have been so easy to continue this if we had persisted in running STARGARD as a separate operation.

Whatever success we had achieved in launching STARGARD it does seem that the concept of a product division could be misplaced in our particular business. Customers' needs are too varied to be identified with any degree of certainty before seeing what an architect has in mind. At that stage it is of course a strength to have a range of solutions available. This could apply even where an advertisement has brought an enquiry for a specific product. Paradoxically it appears that the way forward is to promote clearly identified products, but once an enquiry is received, to sell all-round craftsmanship and solutions to individual problems.

How integrated was our marketing?

As has been said a modest success was recorded in this instance. STARGARD made a significant contribution to growth and played a substantial part in survival, when this became the only game on offer. Things might have been otherwise if we had got everything right or, alternatively, if we had made some major errors. An attempt to summarize what went wrong and what went right, and to see just how integrated our marketing was, must now be made. This is not easy. It is true that I was an observer of all that happened, over a period of some years. Yet I was hardly an impartial observer. Once Harry Watson was firmly in charge my time with the company was little more than a day a month, but that day was spent not as a consultant, but as a participant. It did however give me a rare opportunity to follow the consequences of decisions made through to a conclusion. Readers may well have made different decisions in the circumstances which prevailed, and produced other results.

What went wrong

We were probably trying to do too many things at once. In itself STARGARD was an easy enough product to introduce, but there were other calls on management attention, and changes being made which would impinge on the STARGARD venture. Plans for expansion overseas and a move to larger premises, which were later dropped, the introduction of computers throughout the organization, measures to improve contract control, the implementation of a quality scheme to BS 5750 were all under way at one time or other throughout this period. The company had also to cope with the strains imposed by a rapidly increasing turnover, followed by an equally rapid decline in the market. In such a situation it was unlikely that everything would go smoothly but there were some errors which might possibly have been avoided.

Confusion of objectives Although the need for a new product to augment Strading was clear enough, efforts to find one were diverted into an attempt to improve the existing product. In the event this did not achieve very much. Of course there is no reason why both objectives could not have been pursued independently of each other, but some confusion and delay did occur.

Incorrect estimates of cost The persistent belief that the product would cost less than it in fact did also served to create confusion. It blurred perceptions of where STARGARD stood in the market and it may have encouraged optimism in forecasting. That is in some doubt, since targets might well have been met but for the unforeseen recession. What is not in doubt is that an exaggerated claim to economy was made in the first sales leaflet produced.

Again this did not seem to deter customers to any extent. All projects were quoted individually and the product soon found a place on its own merits. Customers seemed to make comparisons with competitive systems rather than with cheaper powder-coated alternatives. But damage was done. The salesman concerned felt pressures on price as a result of the claim made, and wasted time trying to compete in situations where there was no hope of success. The second version of the leaflet put matters right by stressing the durability of a product which might cost more initially, but this came too late to boost morale which was by then under assault from other directions.

Separation The establishment of a separate unit in one way enhanced integration. Sales, estimating, drawing and production facilities were all together under one roof. Nevertheless the classic error discussed in Chapter 2 had been made, and as soon as parts of the work had to be handled in the main factory, the problems of isolation became acute.

It may be that the error lay in believing that more space was needed, when later measures taken to streamline operations rendered it unnecessary. Certainly the difficulties of handling a rapidly rising turnover in a small, detached unit were not foreseen. The rapidity with which high morale was subverted may have had something to do with the personalities involved, but it was not anticipated and should have been.

What went well

Fortunately more went well than went astray, but that should not serve to excuse the making of two quite fundamental mistakes. They show that however familiar one may be with the principles involved, the pressures of the moment or the persuasions of others can prevail. Indeed only the most dogmatic of managers could be immune to them, and such managers would have little chance of integrating anything.

A strategy based on information The basic strategy was sound, and was based on a wide spread of information. The company's own internal analyses, a detailed study of competitors' accounts and a formal market survey all pointed in the same direction: there was scope for expansion and the best way of avoiding the limitations of the custom-built market was to introduce a new system.

Market segmentation Judgements about the receptiveness of the public sector were correct, although as time went on it became clear that STARGARD had a wider appeal and that promotional efforts should reflect this.

Market acceptance tests No untried assumptions were made about the acceptability of any of the products considered. In every case they were subjected to tests which were conducted without bias. This eliminated alternatives and indicated that STARGARD would be well received when launched.

Sales promotion Literature was prepared in line with marketing objectives and proved effective. Advertising was assessed at every stage and adjusted to maintain enquiries at what was seen to be the optimum level. Salesmen and estimators were closely involved in the design of sales aids to ensure these would work as useful marketing tools.

Coordination of marketing effort Initially there was a pioneering spirit and close coordination among members of a small team. After the separate unit was abandoned this had to be maintained on a more systematic basis. Monthly meetings were held at which all aspects of marketing were discussed. Estimators maintained lists of 'gold star' prospects from whom business might be expected. The salesman was available to call on selected architects and contractors and offer suggestions that might further the sale. Conversion statistics were studied with care and improving ratios bore witness to the success of the methods used.

Coordination of effort with production and the drawing office had to be established afresh when the separate unit was abandoned. That this went as smoothly as it did was due in part to efforts to improve these aspects over the whole product range. The production manager was fully aware of the marketing situation and responded positively to the threat of recession. Customers were welcomed in the workshop, samples were prepared as required and performance targets treated with great respect.

Product and pricing discipline STARGARD maintained its profitability throughout the whole period from the launch. Price discipline was strong and survived disappointment at the failure to meet the original cost expectations. The company's reaction to pressure from customers was to offer some tangible alternative rather than simply to reduce price. In this way it was possible to compete and at the same time retain a reputation for integrity and craftsmanship.

The integration of Sales and Production where delivery promises were concerned was vital. Under the pressures of recession main contractors were behaving quite ruthlessly to any supplier who failed to perform. Time was given to studying factory work loads and each order was slotted in with care. STARGARD was of course particularly suited to filling gaps as they occurred, so very short deliveries could be offered, on occasion.

An untidy world Any attempt to draw an organization chart of the company at any stage of the period that has been considered would have run into difficulty. Small firms are seldom tidy in this respect and managers may have more than one set of responsibilities. Marketing, for example, was handled by the managing director, a very part-time adviser, one salesman and a team of estimators, with occasional help from other people including the production manager. But it worked, largely because of the degree to which efforts were integrated. Everyone knew what was happening and was prepared to measure the results of initiatives taken. Effort could then easily be directed to where it would be likely to produce the best return. Organization charts do not bring about a communal will to succeed in difficult times. Leadership is however highly relevant, and the role of the managing director in securing an integrated approach will be vital whatever the size of the organization. This will be considered in greater detail in Chapter 8.

Questions and action points for decision takers

The purpose of a case study is to stimulate thought around and about a real-life situation. It cannot be known in advance what aspects of the story recounted in Chapter 7 will appear relevant to readers. To select items for attention could therefore work against the objective of this chapter. In summarizing what appeared to go right or wrong I have already moved beyond a simple account of happenings, and would not wish to go further than this. The reader is invited to construct a personal list of points of interest. Purely as an example, here are two that occurred to Harry Watson.

In launching a new product, has the impact of other developments planned for the company been fully considered?

In forecasting sales, what assumptions have been made about the peaks and troughs of order input?

8

The open company
Elements in effective integration

For a chief executive marketing is not always the top priority. At any given time other matters may be demanding more urgent attention, debt collection, for example, or legal problems over premises, or cost reduction in the factory. It is no use concentrating effort on marketing if you have run out of money, or have no roof over your head, or if the product has priced itself out of all credibility. The realization that there may be other claims on the chief's time, and *that these claims are valid,* is salutary for marketing managers. In itself it constitutes a step towards the integration of effort, because marketing plans made in the context of what is happening elsewhere in the firm are more likely to succeed than those made in isolation.

Yet there is a marketing dimension to every decision made, which means that, whatever the immediate priority, marketing should never be entirely absent from a managing director's thoughts. The man or woman at the top is therefore in the prime position to promote the integration of marketing into the fabric of the company, regardless of whether he or she has come from a marketing background. So we need to see what positive steps someone who may not have personal experience in every aspect of the craft can take to make it all happen.

First we should dispose of one cure-all method favoured by government departments, nationalized industries and many large commercial organizations, which can be summarized as 'a clear delegation of responsibilities'. The concept is embodied in organization charts, terms of reference, regular meetings, committees and subcommittees, reports and forms of many different kinds. Any or all of these may be necessary, but do not, of themselves guarantee integration of effort. At times they can make it harder to achieve, because formal structures create defensive walls for those so minded.

The problems we have identified in previous chapters are essentially problems of attitude. Measures to promote integration have in consequence to be designed to impinge on attitudes throughout the company.

An examination of the remedies suggested so far will indicate that they can be grouped under two main headings:

- measurement
- communication.

Neither is the sole responsibility of the chief executive. The whole thrust of the argument has been towards greater involvement on the part of many more people. But the person in charge can do much to see that the tools of integration are used effectively.

Measurement for all

Within the marketing department itself what has been advocated is largely an extension of what should be normal practice. Setting objectives and measuring results against them is the very stuff of marketing. The skill lies in selecting the right objectives, making sure they are common to all marketing functions, and devising ways of measurement that are accepted as meaningful by those actually doing the work. It has been suggested that areas which may have escaped measurement in the past, such as PR and certain forms of advertising, should be given close attention. Nothing too rigid or black and white has been proposed. Several different ways of assessing results may be used simultaneously to create a clearer picture of the overall situation, and a degree of approximation is in some cases unavoidable. Furthermore, as objectives change, new ways of measurement may have to be devised.

The cause of integration is advanced – and the efficiency of the company as a whole improved – if departments outside marketing are also set objectives and their results assessed in an appropriate fashion. This is natural enough in some areas such as production performance, but should be extended as widely as possible. Everyone has a job to do, and needs some indication of whether it is producing worthwhile results. What is being recommended is not a formal 'Management by Objectives' scheme: such schemes are usually productive in their first year but fade in effectiveness thereafter. We are looking for measurements of everyday activity and productivity that can become a permanent part of business life, rather than a one-off exercise.

The managing director has the job of seeing that the various objectives set and standards applied are not at variance with each other, and that they are all related to the needs of the market. It is not always an easy task. Cost reduction exercises in the factory might undermine the attractiveness of the product; efficiency in debt collecting, if conducted with a heavy hand, could alienate loyal customers. Some of the potential conflicts between departments have been identified in previous chapters, and it has been argued that these are not simply clashes of personality, but stem from attitudes related to the nature of the work which Development, Production or Accounts undertake.

The very act of measurement itself, if it is applied clumsily, can be counter-productive. The jobs people do are sometimes complex and in selecting certain aspects for attention, other sides may be forgotten. A rigid system of norms for performance tends to encourage barrack room lawyers. The norm then becomes the maximum that can be expected and a cloak for failure in other respects.

In an open company measurement is simply recognizing that people are trying to achieve various goals and accepting that the progress they make towards their objectives should be known as widely as possible. If the goals are worth while no one is going to succeed all the time. Knowing as a simple matter of fact what has been achieved and what has not clears the way for further advances. Knowledge of what other departments are doing, and attempting to do, enables potential conflicts to be resolved at an early stage. Measurement therefore needs to be linked to good communication, if it is to be fully effective.

Communication all round

The need for Marketing to explain to other departments what it is trying to accomplish has been a common thread throughout this book. To set out the basis on which sales forecasts are made, for example, implies a degree of openness which challenges both the competence and the powers of persuasion of marketing managers. Making sure that findings of market research are widely known, and understood, again involves letting others see how marketing works. Establishing product and delivery disciplines requires a clear understanding between marketing and production managers. There are then many steps that can be taken on the initiative of individual departmental managers.

It would however be optimistic to expect that a high level of integration will be reached without the encouragement of the chief executive. Freedom of communication throughout the company will be strongly influenced by the attitude shown at the top.

Communication, just as much as measurement, is not enhanced by reliance on a rigidly systematized approach. Marketing meetings, management meetings, development meetings and coordinating meetings of all kinds may well be necessary. They are not, however, likely to be sufficient if they are the only occasions on which the parties involved speak to each other. Furthermore a formal structure of meetings may well ignore the communication needs of those who are not invited to attend. Outside the 'charmed circle' of decision-makers may be others who feel that their views are being neglected.

It would seem that neither of the tools of use in furthering the integration of marketing effort, measurement and communication, is sufficient in itself or particularly easy to use. There are no set routines or management techniques that will produce the desired result automatically. A marketing manager with an understanding of what his or her craft really demands can do much to secure unanimity, but the openness which is a condition of success cannot be established unless the managing director clears the way for it.

An open company

In an open company measurement is merely recognition of the facts of a situation, which serves to stimulate thought about alternative courses of action. Communication is simply the right of all employees to know what is happening and where the company is going. In such circumstances it is relatively easy to keep the needs of customers in the front of all minds, and integrated marketing becomes a practical proposition. Whether this appears as a remote ideal or an everyday experience depends on the management style of the chief executive.

A desire for efficiency is often at the root of restrictions on openness and failure to communicate throughout the company. Senior managers are under pressure to fit in more hours than the day contains. So they are taught that time must not be wasted, and armed with 'personal organizers' and secretaries to ensure that all goes to programme. The secretaries are placed in front of the office door to see that there are no unplanned intrusions, and minions troop in and out to order, encouraged to say their piece economically and make way for the next priority. Thus chief executives are presented, at their own request, with a series of half-truths, and have to use their native wits and experience to decide which to accept as a basis for action.

Sometimes they recognize this as a problem. Then they may emerge to look around their various departments and ask pertinent questions. That is perhaps the most fundamental step that can be taken to counteract the effects of self-imposed isolation. Whether it succeeds or not depends on how the questions are asked. If a chief executive is normally inaccessible a sudden foray into the offices of underlings is more likely to produce fear than an open response. So the answers to questions may be those it is thought the boss would most like to hear. To get beyond this defensive reaction more questions must be put, so what you have is not communication but interrogation.

Some senior managers try to compensate for this by adopting a more paternalistic stance. They take a personal interest in employees. With a good memory or a discreet filing system it is possible to associate individuals with husbands or wives, families or hobbies, and make reference to them as an opener. Now I would not argue against taking a genuine interest in people, nor against asking pertinent questions, it is just that something more has to be given.

The company matters to all its members, as much as it does to its chief executive. What is happening in the organization, what its current objectives are, where it is seeing possibilities for the future: these are the topics of conversation if two-way communication is desired. In talking about such matters freely the chief executive is crediting others with an equal interest in the well-being of the firm, and implicitly inviting them to contribute whatever they have to give. At the same time a standard of openness is being set for other managers to follow. This is why management style is so important, because in the climate thus created integrated marketing can be achieved with no more than what we have seen to be routine difficulty.

Exactly how much time should be spent in communicating in this way cannot be prescribed. A certain amount of untidiness may be the price of releasing more of the energies of other members of staff. Such experience as I have would indicate that the time available for making real decisions will not be greatly eroded, and the decisions themselves will be founded on better information. The alternative of minimum trust, and information doled out on a 'need to know' basis, leads logically to the chief executive making every decision personally, after long and frustrating interrogation of unwilling witnesses, which is hardly a recipe for efficiency. The test of openness is that people come to you with problems and ideas before you have to question them.

Security aspects

What about confidential information? Naturally it all depends on what is deemed to be confidential. An instinctive desire to protect 'secrets' seems almost universal. It is not only large companies that keep their employees in the dark. Small firms, especially where the chief executive is also the owner or part-owner, are frequently the worst in this respect. The tradition of master and servant lingers on.

Clearly there are security aspects that need to be addressed. If, for example, there were to be a genuine product innovation which could provide a real advantage over competition, it might be wise not to give competitors advanced notice of it. But even in such circumstances the dangers of a fast reaction from rivals need to be weighed against the dangers of failing to check that the product is really right for the market and that everyone in the firm is well briefed to make a success of it.

Tight security is often maintained over far less sensitive aspects of a company's activity, so that facts and figures that would help to promote openness and understanding are given a very restricted circulation. It may help in all cases of this kind to ask what your most powerful competitors would do if they had access to your figures or even knew what you were planning. Often, but not always, there is very little they could or would do in the short term, except pursue their own strategies as vigorously as possible.

Internal personnel changes are another matter. Here there is a case for discretion if not for secrecy. If promotions are pending, or a reshuffle of responsibilities, it is asking too much of human nature to canvass the possibilities around those likely to be affected adversely. There is everything to be said for handling such matters expeditiously and explaining the decisions made thereafter.

Selecting a marketing manager

A chief executive may promote the integration of marketing in another, very direct way, that is, in selecting a marketing manager. For we have by now made a significant change to the job specification for this post. What is being sought is not just someone who is skilled in the craft of marketing, but someone who will act in such a way that marketing becomes an integral part of the company with its activities fully coordinated with those of other departments.

This would seem to rule out whiz-kids high on ego and low on empathy, but it is to be hoped that you would not be interested in them in any case. What is wanted is evidence of craftsmanship in past appointments and of a craft approach to what may be new tasks. Few potential managers are likely to have had time to master all aspects of marketing. How a job has been tackled is therefore as important as the results claimed, because it is the only available pointer to how future work will be approached.

This is not the place for a detailed discourse on selection techniques, but in the many interviews I have conducted for marketing appointments at all levels I found the answers given to one particular question revealing. Whether previous experience had been wide or fairly limited, I would take a well-defined slice of it and ask: 'And what did you most enjoy about that (job, activity, university course, etc)?' It was surprising, and disconcerting, how often such a question elicited a blank stare. Perhaps jobs are not meant to be enjoyed. But real craftsmen do enjoy their work, and enjoy learning and practising new skills within their chosen trade. Furthermore, provided they are also communicators, such people are more likely to spread their enthusiasm throughout the company.

In a small company it is likely that there will be gaps in the experience of candidates for the marketing job. If these are too great the job may have to be shared by two or even more people undertaking different aspects of it. The chief executive may then have to play a major role in marketing, as well as to see that all aspects of it are fully integrated. One purpose in selecting a small firm's case study for Chapter 7, was to show that this is possible, even for a managing director with little previous experience of the craft. In an open company the learning curve can be quite steep, because everyone contributes towards making it so, and shares in the sense of achievement that follows.

Questions and action points for decision takers

Measurement

How is the performance of each department measured?

What objectives have been set in each case?

Have potential conflicts been identified and eliminated?

Are all objectives related to the needs of the market?

Communication

Have each department's objectives been discussed with the heads of other departments?

Are they known throughout the company?

Are performance figures known and discussed throughout the company?

Does your own management style encourage openness in others?

Do people come to you with problems and ideas before you question them?

What facts and figures are kept secret?

Is it necessary that they should all be treated in this way?

Marketing manager

Have you drawn up a specification for a marketing manager?

How will you look for signs of ability to integrate the marketing function?

If the job has to be split, what aspects of marketing do you feel competent to handle yourself?

Index